EDNA'S CIRCLE:

Edna Staebler's Century of Friendships

EDNA'S CIRCLE:

Edna Staebler's Century of Friendships

by

Nancy Silcox

Photography credits:
My thanks go to those Edna-friends who provided me with the photos that appear in this book. They were all treasures and I regret that space did not allow me to use all of those forwarded to me. Those included came from: *Salome Bearinger, Sheila Chaffecombe, Madelene Dewar, Jim Hertel (WLU), Teresa Huegel, Ivan Kraemer, Barbara Naylor, Veronica Ross, Irene Schmidt, Peter Etril Snyder, Kevin Thomason, Pat Zehr. A special thanks to Simon Wilson whose stunning image of Edna is on the cover.*

Edna's Circle: Edna Staebler's Century of Friendships

ISBN 978-0-9730289-2-8

Design by Karl Griffiths-Fulton, Pandora Press, Kitchener, Canada.

Support for this project was greatly received from:

The Milton R. Good Foundation

 Waterloo Regional Heritage Foundation

If a man does not make new acquaintance as he advances through life, he will soon find himself left alone. A man, Sir, should keep his friendship in constant repair.

Samuel Johnson

Contents

Acknowledgements

A number of people were invaluable in assisting me to write this book. They are: (in no particular order) Susan Chilton of the *Record* and Carol Jankowski of *Grand Magazine*; Karen Ball-Pyatt (KPL); Wilmot Mayor Wayne Roth; Jim Hertel (WLU); Ivan Kraemer; Pat Zehr; Barbara Naylor; Veronica Ross; Sheila Chaffecombe; Irene Schmidt; Dr. Paul Tiessen; Nancy Martin; Eva Bauman and my friend Hilde Slezak for her gifts at the outset of this project of *To Experience Wonder: Edna Staebler: A Life; and Must Write: Edna Staebler's Diaries*.

I am grateful to the late June Callwood who, despite her illness called and wrote to pass on her reminiscences of Edna. Very deep thanks to Kevin Thomason for his encouragement and assistance throughout the progress of the book.

My acknowledgement would not be complete without a huge thank you to my husband Louis who "mopped up" as my brain turned to jelly in the closing weeks of completing the book.

And finally, I'd like to thank those who have supported this project financially. These partnerships mean my goal of delivering all book profits to charities that Edna supported will be realized. First, thanks to Joe and Stephanie Mancini whose expertise in maneuvering through the grant application process was paramount in its positive outcome. Also to Kim Jernigan, who added *The New Quarterly's* voice of support to the application. To the Milton R. Good Foundation, and its spokesman James Good, I am deeply grateful for giving generous support to the book. As well, I'd like to thank the Waterloo Regional Heritage Foundation who not only generously supported me, but responded to my request in "record" time.

Note to Readers:
Edna Staebler's circle of friends was an immense one, and their accumulated stories would surely have filled several books. In

choosing the 41 voices that the reader will hear in *Edna's Circle*, I have surely left "41 x10" stories untold.

My task in choosing spokespersons for organizations that benefited from Edna's philanthropy was no less difficult. In the end, time and space allowed me to feature only 3 that Edna assisted financially. They are: Wilfrid Laurier University, The Working Centre and St. John's Kitchen, and *The New Quarterly*.

Other beneficiaries not profiled include: The United Way, the Kitchener Public Library, Joseph Schneider Haus, the Humane Society, and the Mennonite Central Committee, as well as several Old Order Mennonite Churches. I am aware that Edna assisted in covering the medical costs of several Old Order Mennonite friends. Those of the Old Order do not usually pay into OHIP; hence their medical expenses are not covered by the province of Ontario and can be very costly.

Nor was Edna's bounty restricted to individuals and organizations in the Kitchener-Waterloo Region. The Cabot High School in Neil's Harbour, Cape Breton Island received a handsome cheque in 2006 to assist them improve a sorely under-funded library. This was a continuation of the ongoing, generous support Edna had provided to Neil's Harbour. In years past, Edna frequently packaged "remaindered" books—her own, those left over from the annual Canadian Federation of University Women Book Sale, and any others she could gather. She then shipped them to The Cabot High School library.

Edna also showed her generosity to many individuals—those close to her and those further removed. Over the course of the year that I sought Edna's stories, I heard from more than one person who had gone to their letter box one day to find an envelope written in a familiarly spidery hand. Inside was a cheque, accompanied only by a brief note that urged them to: "Enjoy," or "Have Fun!" The benefactor? Edna Staebler.

Perhaps no one will ever know the full extent of Edna's generosity.

Preface

My introduction to Edna Staebler came in the summer of 1999. I was in the concluding stages of writing my first book, *Roads of the Heart*, a series of 50 biographies of people with ties to the Waterloo Region—Wilmot Township to be precise—who had taken "the road less traveled" in their personal and professional lives. An acquaintance asked me if I had yet interviewed Edna Staebler for the book. I replied that I hadn't, and explained why that was so.

While I was fully aware that Edna lived in the Township (who in Waterloo Region didn't know that Edna lived at Sunfish Lake?), and I would have been honoured to include her in *Roads*, as a stranger and first-time author, I had felt intimidated to ring up such an esteemed Canadian. Secondly, I knew little about Edna, save that she was of a great age—past her 90th birthday. Was she well? Would she be up for an interview?

This rationale sent my interrogator into gales of laughter. "Edna at 93 is sharper than most people 30 years younger," she advised. And, as for my notion of Edna's fame pre-disposing her to "celebrity airs," I was told that one couldn't find a less-intimidating woman—celebrity or not—on the face of the earth. But to assuage my uncertainties about contacting Edna personally, she would make the introductory call.

Several days later, my phone rang and a caller, identifying herself as Edna Staebler invited me over for a chat. Of course, she would be delighted to take part in my book. She always liked to make time for young writers. When could I come? Just like that!

And so, my friendship with Edna Staebler began.

Certain memories of that hot August afternoon with Edna remain vivid. I recall her gait; this was no shuffling nonagenarian, dependant on a walker or cane for security.

Edna moved quickly and surely around the room, with a spring in her step. Her face, too, belied her years. It had a quality of serenity—smooth and clear, without deep lines. The woman sitting across from me seemed ageless.

I remember also her open friendliness with me, a stranger whom she had only just met. Edna talked freely of her own life story, including her unhappy marriage and eventual divorce. Yet far from seeming indiscrete, Edna's words spoke only of a woman who intuitively trusted people with her confidences.

One Visit is Not Enough

I left that first visit asking if I might return. One "telling" had hardly scratched the surface of her long and celebrated life. And so, some days later, we met once more, in that cozy cottage on the shores of Sunfish Lake, surrounded by Edna's memories— her books, her paintings, her photographs and her letters. Each one of them told a story and combined to paint a portrait of this singular woman, born in the days when Kitchener was called Berlin; in the years before Canada first went to war; before women could vote, indeed, before women were considered persons.

My interviews now concluded, I left that day, knowing I would return again, and again. Over the next 4 years, long after my book was printed and sold, I regularly made time to visit Edna—not out of a sense of duty to keep company with an elderly "neighbour," but out of desire. And as I came to know her better, I realized there were dozens, scores, even hundreds of folk who, like me, made the trek regularly to Sunfish Lake and Edna Staebler.

Keeping Track of Them All

I soon learned that scheduling a visit with Edna took some long-range planning. She kept track of her many visitors on the current year's edition of the "Milk Calendar," a publication, it appeared, for cooks and social types alike. "The white spaces for each day of the week are big enough for me to write everyone down," she offered, and added: "so why buy a fancy one at the stationery store?" I chuckled to myself remembering my own grandmother's "save everything for a rainy day" philosophy.

Even then, I couldn't be certain that a visit with Edna would be a tête-à-tête. Edna never gave the cold shoulder to "drop-ins." Unexpected visitors were as welcome as scheduled callers. At first, jealous of sharing my special "Edna time" with others, soon I viewed this serendipitously, as an opportunity to meet the people who made up Edna's world. I learned too that Edna delighted in introducing callers to callers. A Romantic at heart, she took credit for the occasional romance that had bloomed after a chance meeting at Sunfish Lake.

Edna's Circle
Before long, I had gained an insight into the "who's who" of Edna's myriad of callers. Some, whom I came to call "the inner circle," comprised 5 or 6 people. These were longtime and trusted friends and confidants—those Edna turned to for support, advice and assistance. They included Edna's next-door neighbour and guardian angel, Kevin Thomason—surely the grandson that Edna never had. Also Barbara Naylor, a friend for over 40 years who found her place there too. Their memories of Edna are included here.

An expansive "middle circle," was made up of regular callers from a wide variety of associations. Some traced their friendship back to Edna's early days at Sunfish; others were longtime neighbours or friends. This grouping also included several Old Order Mennonite friends, writing associates and the odd representative of organizations to which Edna had donated money. How many fit into this "cluster?" 50? 100? Or more? Each time I visited Edna, I learned the name of someone new.

Further from the Edna-vortex were her fans—people who might have telephoned (her name was in the phone book for all to see, after all!) to tell her personally how much her *Schmecks* cookbooks had meant to them. Others might have come to seek an autograph; or to pass on a personal "hello; I think you are wonderful." University students also dropped by, coming to thank Edna for the awards she funded at Wilfrid Laurier University.[1] A regular *coterie* of journalists, reporters, radio personalities and other media types who were looking for a story on a legend came to call too. Yes, Edna's Milk Calendar was always full.

A Casual Observation
It was during a prized chat for two that I casually made a suggestion. "Edna," I offered, "you have so many fascinating callers—writers who want to interview you; film makers who want to film you; university presidents who want to thank you for your donations; fans who want you to sign their *Schmecks* cookbooks.... Someone should write a book about them."

Edna's keen eyes sparkled at my suggestion, and aware that I was looking for a new writing project, enthusiastically volunteered me for the job! I was flattered, but gave little more thought to the notion. And time passed.

A Move from Sunfish
Edna's ill-health and subsequent move to Beechwood Manor in the spring of 2003 resulted in changes to her regulated social calendar. Previously, Edna had been able to schedule her callers; now many dropped in unannounced. It was often "Standing Room Only" in Edna's small room.

And while it was obvious that she prized her callers as a lifeline, I noticed how quickly Edna tired. Beechwood Manor staff had witnessed the same, and decided that action was needed. A sign made an appearance on Edna's door advising that her rest time was in the early afternoon.

Beechwood Administrator, Ruth Deyarmond, whose stories of Edna at Beechwood are found within this book, noted that her staffs' fierce protectiveness of Edna was the rationale behind the restrictions. A former Beechwood Manor employee, Sheila Chaffecombe offers Edna's spirited reaction to the turning back of one visitor—and an important one at that.

Moving to More Care
In 2005, Columbia Forest Long-Term Care became Edna's last home. She was now inching toward her 100th birthday, and visitors continued to flock to her. Columbia Forest needed to follow Beechwood Manor's example in "crowd control."

I now visited Edna less frequently, making a conscious decision to be one less person in her room. Thinking that I wouldn't be missed, I only learned after her death that she felt a slight. I sorely regret my altruistic decision now.

My last visit to Edna was in the summer of 2006. Both animal lovers, she and I talked for almost an hour about the pets we both had loved. Edna regaled me with tales of Buddy the Car-Hopping Pooch, and Cicely, the Bird Assassin. With her permission, I taped our conversation and I treasure it as a poignant souvenir of our brief friendship.

Tributes Pour In
Edna passed away on September 12, 2006. She was surrounded by the closest of her "circle," including Kevin and Barbara. The cat, Oliver, whom Edna had adopted (some say it the other way round!) lay on the bed as Edna's bonds slipped the earth. A memorial for her, later held at Wilfrid Laurier University was an opportunity for friends, neighbours, benefactors and colleagues to share their memories.

Tributes came also from across the country. On the day following Edna's death, CBC Radio devoted much of its morning hour to replaying earlier recorded interviews with Edna and various CBC radio personalities, including Peter Gzowski. A delightful anecdote in this book, contributed by Barbara Naylor calls to mind a Staebler-Gzowski interview from some years past.

In those days following her death, as I heard, read and reflected on the words of praise, gratitude and love for the remarkable Edna Staebler, the long-forgotten memory of our conversation regarding her "circle of friends" re-visited me. And so the seeds of this book were born.

Brush Strokes Paint a Picture

This would be no biography of the indomitable Edna, as had been carefully and sensitively written by Kitchener writer, Veronica Ross, in *To Experience Wonder: Edna Staebler: A Life*. My study would metaphorically take the form of a composite portrait of Edna Louise Staebler. The contributing "artists"—drawn from Edna's vast circle of friends, fans and admirers would be invited to add their brush strokes to complete the image.

But how to chose only 40 "artists" (I saw that figure as an ideal number) of the hundreds who had known, loved and admired Edna Staebler? The task would be a difficult one, to be sure.

Edna's Heart and Soul

In the end, I called on only 2 of Edna's "inner circle" to add their colour. Their insightful memories of a dear friend would form the "soul," of the portrait. I searched also for those whose intimacy with Edna had been less substantial—-her publishers, writing colleagues, business associates, neighbours, long-time friends and newer ones. These individuals would paint Edna's "face and body." I wished also to add the "background details" of several of Edna's fans. But how to find them? My solution came with a call to Andrea Bailey, editor of the *Waterloo Chronicle* newspaper. Might she be willing to write a story on "Edna's Circle," and invite anyone who had memories of Edna to make themselves known to me? It was an inspired idea, for I received several charming stories, which are included in the book.

Almost a year after my journey began, with over 40 "contributors" contacted and convinced to add their own colour to "Edna's Circle," my book reached its happy conclusion. And while I am satisfied that their hues are vibrant, deep and strong, I know that my portrait of Edna cannot be called complete. For each person who applied their brushstrokes, uncounted other details remain unrealized.

It has been, at times, an exhilarating, intriguing, and joyful experience—but not one without its sorrow and poignancy. I carry a deep regret that my visits to Edna in the latter stages of her life were few. And so, this book is my apology to her.

As author and editor, I too feel a need to add my small brush strokes to Edna's portrait. And while my story is neither profound nor insightful, it is a delightful one, and adds substance to Edna's reputation as a woman who enjoyed having fun—a "scallywag," who was not above a whit of mischievousness.

Mice Gone Missing!
Edna was a Renaissance Woman. Her wide-ranging *curriculum vitae* might have included the descriptions: writer, cook, gardener, nature lover, world traveler, philanthropist and... knitter. But no crafter of baby booties or wooly sweaters and sox was she. Edna knit "mice."

In Peterborough, Edna's sister Ruby had begun a "cottage industry." Ruby's products were hand-knitted cat toys, fashioned as life-size mice, each sporting a cat-captivating long tail, and stuffed with premium catnip. Edna had volunteered to be one of her sister's knitters. With needles clacking, she could complete several mice in the course of an afternoon while visiting, or keeping an eye on television in the evening.

When she'd done sufficient to warrant a package—several dozen, Edna would mail them to Ruby for stuffing and finishing. Marketed as "Edna's Mice" (a clever bit of celebrity marketing there), the novelty was then sold at pet-stores throughout the K-W and Peterborough areas. A favourite of cat-lovers in both centers, the mice flew off the shelves almost as fast as they arrived.

One day when I came to Sunfish for a visit, I found Edna "in a lather." A shipment of the mice had gone astray, courtesy of Canada Post! Alerted to their disappearance by Ruby, Edna had contacted the "dead letter" office at the Kitchener Post Office to begin the search for the missing rodents.

After being passed from one postal employee to another, she finally reached someone who would listen to her story. Edna takes the tale from here:

> "So I said to the guy on the phone that a parcel I'd sent to my sister in Peterborough had gone missing."
>
> "And he said: 'what's in the parcel, ma'am?'"
>
> "And I said: 'Mice; about 3 dozen of them.'"
>
> " 'Mice! Geez' lady, what are you doing sending mice in the mail?' He fairly bellowed at me!"
>
> "To which I replied: 'Well, they weren't the full mouse, just the skins.' "
>
> "I wanted to pull his leg and I did have him going for awhile," she said, with a twinkle in her eye.

Didn't you just love that Edna?

Nancy Silcox
New Hamburg
July 2007.

---

1. Edna gave two annual scholarships to WLU students; one in the name of her friend Gerry Noonan; the other to recognize writer George Blackburn, a friend and former winner of the Edna Staebler Award for Creative Nonfiction.

EDNA:
THE EARLY YEARS

*I remember my youth and the feeling
that will never come back anymore —
the feeling that I could last forever,
outlast the sea, the earth an all men;
the deceitful feeling that lures us on
to joys, perils, to love, to vain effort...*

Joseph Conrad
Youth

Edna: the Early Years

Arthur Prudham
"Mother had volunteered...to be a 'buddy' to one of the new first-year students. Her 'buddy' was Edna Cress."

Win Shantz
"With a good-natured laugh, Edna suggested it be served as 'spoon cake,' like pudding. Everyone found it funny."

Marjorie Barber
"Edna had the ability to laugh at herself. She didn't take herself totally seriously..."

Arthur Prudham
for
Helen Prudham (nee Kay)

Edna Cress (Staebler) graduated from Kitchener Collegiate Institute and Vocational School (K.C.I.) in 1926. She was 20 years of age. Although she didn't consider herself a scholar, Edna wanted to continue on to university. The University of Toronto was where she had chosen to study. She said:

> "Neither of my parents had gone to university before me; neither did my two younger sisters after me. But I had always wanted to go to university. I wanted to get away from home and I liked learning new things. But my parents told me that if I failed any courses, I'd be finished and would come home."[1]

Her parents' threat spurred her on to keep her academic record spotless:

> "I knew what the alternative to university would be— sitting around every afternoon playing bridge and going to I.O.D.E. meetings. And I sure didn't want to get into that kind of boring life! "[2]

In Anne Rochon Ford's book, A Path Not Strewn with Roses; One Hundred Years of Women at the University of Toronto, 1884-1984, *she observed that: "Women who attended university in the early years of this century were very exceptional people....*[3]

Indeed, in 1926, as Edna joined her freshman class, at U. of T., there were scant few women enrolled in the Faculties of Science and Mathematics; only a handful were registered in the Arts and Humanities. Nor were women well represented as faculty members. While the university did employ one or two women as teachers, they did not rise beyond the status of Associate Professor.

When women faculty married, their positions were terminated. In 1931, University President Sir Robert Falconer issued a directive to various faculties. He decreed that: "It is undesirable to employ married women in the University setting."[4]

Edna had enrolled in a Pass (General) Arts program at University College, University of Toronto, and had selected a wide variety of first year classes: English Literature, French, Psychology, Zoology and Religious Knowledge. She was disappointed that there were no courses offered in writing, as becoming a writer had been her lifelong goal.

> "I had always wanted to be a writer—even when I was a little girl, imagining that I was the heroine of every story I read. But at that point I thought that to write about exciting adventures, you had to have experienced them. I had hoped to find out how to write at university."[5]

A Home Away From Home

Queen's Hall would be Edna's home away from home for the next year. In 1905, the University had acquired the former home on the corner of Queen's Park and College Streets, situated close to the campus. When Edna arrived in September 1926, Queen's Hall was the university's only residence for female students.

It was here that her path would cross with that of Miss Helen Kay of Stratford. The two women would strike up a friendship which would continue over the next 75 years.

Arthur Prudham, of Waterloo, recalls his mother, Helen (Kay) Prudham talking of her university days and of her friendship with Edna Cress. His information sheds some light on life for female University of Toronto students in the "Roaring 20's."

Mother had gone to university at 18. She was in her second year of studies, and living in Queen's Hall when Edna arrived in 1926. Mother called her residence "board and keep" and she paid $38.50 a month to live there.

Most students moved out of residence after their first year, but Mother remained there for all 4 of her university years. She had volunteered (or perhaps been offered reduced "board and keep") to be a "buddy" to one of the new first-year students. That meant showing them the ropes, answering their questions, helping them over the transition from home to living away, and other such duties. Mother's "buddy" was Edna Cress, of Kitchener. I believe that they became friends over that year and remained friends, although not close ones, from then on.

Edna's own memories of residence life are positive ones.

"Oh, living in residence was wonderful. I loved the freedom of being away from home and meeting all sorts of interesting people. Some of the girls I met there remained friends long after I finished university." [6]

So Much to Offer in Toronto

Classes, at least for undergraduate Arts students were only in the mornings. Afternoons were kept for studying and attending cultural events. With a desire to become a teacher, Helen Kay burned the midnight oil, studying hard and writing essays. As a History and English double major, she must surely have had her work cut out for her in the latter chore.

By her own admission, Edna found some difficulty getting down to the task at hand. A diary entry shows her frustration with at least the writing part of academics:

"Wrote essay. I hate writing rotten essays. It makes me feel so terrible and guilty. I get all sorts of beautiful thoughts and know exactly what should be there, and can always tell what doesn't sound right, but somehow I never can write what I like to."[7]

Edna's thoughts centre more on life and love:

"...go on writing and stop being such a damned fool... that it was not I, or Cicely (sic) who mattered, but love itself: not my suffering that must be eased, but love that must be served. That only by love do we come to an understanding of the truth."[8]

Social outings also took up Edna's afternoons. She enjoyed attending afternoon concerts and live theatre at the Royal Alexandra and Massey Hall. She also took in shopping at the big Simpson's and Eaton's Department stores along Yonge Street. Edna might have looked regularly, but she wasn't a big buyer, preferring to hand sew most of her wardrobe.

Her fun-loving and lively personality made her a popular girl with members of the opposite sex.

"Yes I had lots of dates at university—but nothing serious; just fun; going to dances and parties. I had a beau in Kitchener and was head over heels in love with him."[9]

An Early Try at Creative Writing

In an attempt to learn how to write, Edna, joined the school's newspaper, The Varsity. *Even by her own admission, her early writing attempts for this publication were not inspired.*

"I wrote a piece for the student newspaper called 'Drinking Buttermilk at the Women's Union.' I can't remember why I chose this or much of anything about it, but it made me realize another thing about writing. Not only did you need to know how to write, but you had to have something important to write about. And it sure wasn't buttermilk!" [10]

Edna's buttermilk story would be the first and only contribution she'd make to The Varsity.

Edna moved out of Queen's Hall at the end of the year and took an apartment with other friends. However, over the next two years she kept in touch with Helen, her former first-year "buddy." In 1929 Helen Kay graduated with an Honours Degree in History and English. Edna earned her degree as well, with a Pass (3 year) Bachelor of Arts.

Life After University

Both women went their separate ways after graduation. Helen enrolled at the Ontario College of Education (OCE) in Toronto. Edna went home to Kitchener to look for a job.

Her first position was at The Kitchener-Waterloo Record. *It saw her keeping track of the revenue collected from customers by* Record *paperboys. She didn't remain on the paper's payroll for long. "I wasn't good at adding,"[11] Edna admitted.*

The Waterloo Trust Company was the next stop on the employment "train." Her job at this establishment would be as a teller. This too was an ill fit. "Nobody could read my handwriting,"[12] Edna volunteered, with a laugh.

After a year in the work-a-day world, and with no satisfaction in sight, Edna decided to try being a teacher. She returned to Toronto and OCE to earn her Bachelor of Education certification. In 1932, she became a qualified teacher and was promptly hired to teach at the small Ingersoll High School, east of London, Ontario.

Once again Edna did not impress her employers and the school board did not renew her contract for the next year. She returned to Kitchener, and after a short stint managing her father's business, the Waterloo Spring Company, she married Keith Staebler. Edna's working days now ended, as she settled, optimistically, into married life.

Over the years, Edna and Helen remained in touch, writing and making the occasional visit. It was as a result of this long association that, over 70 years later, Helen's son Arthur met his mother's old friend.

As Christmas approached, Mother and Edna had always exchanged Christmas letters. But by 1999, Mother's health was such that she went into a nursing home. Edna's letter to her old university friend arrived on schedule. She had added a personal touch, too, recommending some books that she thought Mother should read. Of course, this letter was never answered.

Several months into the New Year, I decided to pay Edna a call explaining to her why Mother had never responded. It was my first trip to Sunfish Lake—but not my last. I liked Edna; she was interesting and fun. It felt good too to continue a relationship that had begun so many years ago.

I usually went out to Sunfish once a season. It became like a "hobby" to me. The warm months were a perfect occasion to ride my bike out from Waterloo. Winter brought with it an opportunity to talk to Edna about birds—which ones had come to her feeder and mine; what was the best feeder to deter the pesky squirrels.

One day when I arrived, Edna's TV aerial had come unhinged and she was perturbed that she couldn't listen to her favourite CBC Radio shows. I volunteered to re-wire it and still remember the malevolent glare I got from her cat, Mally, during the reconstruction.

I look back on those visits to Sunfish very fondly. Edna was a great conversationalist and she could talk about pretty well everything: current events, travel, interesting people, cats, birds, books, food and so on. No wonder she had so many visitors; no wonder I looked forward to making the trek myself. Edna was good to know.

Arthur Prudham
Waterloo
November 2006

---

1. Unless otherwise noted, all information on Edna's Staebler's school life, including her years at the University of Toronto was gathered during an interview with the author in August, 1999.

2. Ibid.

3. Anne Rochon Ford, *A Path Not Strewn with Roses; One Hundred Years of Women at the University of Toronto. 1884-1984* (Toronto: University of Toronto Press, 1985),p. 45.

4. Rochon Ford, p. 12.

5. Interview with Edna Staebler, August 1999.

6. Ibid.

7. *Must Write: Edna Staebler's Diaries*, ed. Christl Verduyn (Waterloo: Wilfrid Laurier Press, 2005), p. 33.

8. Ibid.

9. Interview Edna Staebler

10. Ibid

11.Ibid

12.Ibid

Winifred (Win) Shantz

Win's first husband Don McLaren had gone to high school with Keith Staebler and the two were friends. Both men also shared a love of music. Don played the violin and banjo and Keith was an accomplished pianist.

From time to time, the McLarens would spend a musical evening at the Staebler home, then a rented house on Patricia Street in Kitchener. The men made music; Edna and Win sat back and enjoyed the show. Win has vivid recollections of these musical evenings.

Don was a decent violinist and banjo picker, but he couldn't hold a candle to Keith. Keith Staebler was the caliber of a professional musician and did perform for audiences from time to time.

The men played anything—classical, show tunes, popular songs of the day. Edna and I would listen appreciatively and join along singing when we could. It was great fun. My memories of Edna from these days were of a happy soul, always "up," who loved entertaining. She usually made cookies for these get-togethers, and we'd enjoy these with coffee when the music took a break.

I had heard that there were problems between Edna and Keith, but I never noticed any friction between them. Still, it seemed a different sort of marriage—different from ours at least. They got along with one another, and cared for one another. I recall running into Keith somewhere and he truly looked awful. I asked him what was wrong and he said that he was so worried about Edna. She had just had a hysterectomy.

But there was never any affection between them, at least anything they ever showed. You never saw a hug, or a pat on the arm—you know the type of fond affection that one usually sees between spouses. It seemed a strange relationship.

A Pinch of this and a Handful of That

After Keith and Edna divorced, and Edna moved to Sunfish Lake, I didn't see much of her. But occasionally I'd drive out to visit her at the cottage. By this time Edna had become a celebrity, thanks to her *Food that Really Schmecks* cookbooks. I recall watching a local television show where she was the guest cook, with hilarious results.

The show was live and Edna had been asked to prepare one of the cake recipes out of her book. It started off pretty ordinary, but soon became funny when Edna started adding ingredients the "Mennonite way" — a pinch of this; a handful of that. Well, when the cake came out of the oven it pretty much was a mess. It hadn't set properly or risen like a cake's supposed to do.

Now, most cooks would be humiliated about such a failure on live TV, but not Edna.

Nothing phased her; she didn't get rattled at all. With a good-natured laugh, she suggested it be served as "spoon cake," like pudding. Everyone found it funny—the host, Edna, the live audience, and no doubt, all the people watching on TV. Best-selling cookbook author or not, a failed recipe for Edna Staebler wasn't such a big deal!

Edna Braves the Storm
Now, this wasn't the only time I encountered Edna's down to earth personality and lack of airs. One day the snow was blowing and wind howling and I hesitated even being out in the storm. But I needed to get some dog food so had ventured out to the pet store. I was at the counter when the door opens and in comes Edna. She was quite the vision: rubber boots, a coat that had seen better days, some sort of woolen toque and carrying a big plastic bag. I wondered what on earth could have brought her in from Sunfish Lake on such a miserable day.

We exchanged comments about the weather and then Edna got to her business. She opened her plastic bag and dumped dozens of little hand-knitted "somethings" on the counter. "Edna, what on earth do you have?" I asked her. In that friendly, chattering manner she had, she told me about her sister, Ruby's business, and her part in it.

Edna was an official mice-knitter for Ruby, and after she'd whipped up a pile of them, she'd send them off to her sister for catnip stuffing. The finished product was then peddled at local pet stores. Apparently, the mice were so popular they flew off store shelves in a matter of hours. "Gotta sell those mice," Edna said.

So it was catnip mice that had brought Edna into town during a snowstorm! And dressing up for the delivery, like the well-off, best-selling author she was, was the furthest thing from her mind. No pretension, no airs, no ego. "Gotta sell those mice!"

How could you *not* love Edna!

Win Shantz
Kitchener
April 2007

Marjorie Barber

In 1957 Marjorie and Bert Barber arrived in Waterloo. Bert had been hired by the fledgling University of Waterloo to begin its Co-Operative program. Over his tenure there, Bert's "baby" would grow to become the largest (and most successful) university level program of its sort in the world.

While Bert was making history Marjorie, a former librarian, was also getting involved in her community.[1] One of her earliest get-acquainted bridges was joining the Waterloo chapter of the Canadian Federation of University Women (CFUW). It was through this organization that she met Edna Staebler. At the time, Edna was writing magazine articles for Maclean's Magazine. *Her fame was still on the horizon.*

Given my background in libraries, and Edna's in writing, we had both volunteered to assist the Waterloo Library Board in their search for a qualified librarian—someone with a degree in Library Science. Up until this time, libraries in Waterloo had been staffed by non-professionals.

Our search would take us to Richmond Hill where we were to interview a candidate. It was a long trip from Waterloo, and gave Edna and I the opportunity to get to know each other. We realized one thing pretty quickly. We both loved to talk! Given this characteristic and the circumstances under which we'd discovered it, we gabbed the entire way to the interview and back home. I'm not sure how much Edna found out about me, but I learned a lot about her.

Edna wasn't shy about talking about her marital problems. I learned about Keith's drinking and philandering, and how their marriage had been very strained for years. And if this wasn't enough, he was now in love with her best friend Helen, whom Edna had taken into their home after Helen's divorce.

I'm not sure that I would have told so much about my personal life as Edna did. But it seemed that she had a real need to share. I later found out that I wasn't the only one in whom Edna had confided. Many of the other women at CFUW were also well aware of the details of what was going on in the unhappy Staebler home, and it was on everybody's lips. I guess it *was* good gossip, and I'll admit I wasn't above the odd "juicy story" too. But it just seemed kind of sad and unfortunate.

Much Better for Both

If I recall correctly, after word got out about the Staebler breakup, not everyone painted Keith totally in black. Some people expressed happiness for *both* Edna and Keith that their lives together had ended. Those who were much closer to them, and who'd known them for a much longer time than I had, saw fault on both sides. Yes, Keith needed to take a large share of the blame for his very public bad treatment of Edna, but Edna was not without fault. They just seemed to make each other miserable together, so it was better for both of them that they went their separate ways.

Keith's friends saw proof of this in the big turnaround in his life after Helen came into the picture. He stopped drinking entirely and went to AA meetings religiously. Keith was a well-liked man in Kitchener-Waterloo, and had a lot of support from a lot of people. They were just glad that he'd found happiness after being miserable for so long.

What Really Galled Edna

Edna and Keith divorced in the early 60's, and Edna sold the house on Simeon Street a while later. I distinctly remember that she was certainly not in love with her new address at Sunfish Lake at first. In fact, losing Keith seemed not to be what had really upset her; it was having to move from her beautiful house on Simeon to the country. That really made her blood boil! Edna told people how much she resented that her mail had to be redirected to her at the lake.

But there were good things that came out of Edna's move to Sunfish, and her spirits soon revived. Of course the best part of the divorce was that Edna's writing career blossomed. I went to visit her one day at the lake and she seemed very happy to be able to come and go as she pleased. She was traveling, writing and earning a paycheck.

The Darned Train!

To give Edna her full dues, despite her pretty public problems, she had always tried to put on a happy face. Edna had the ability to laugh at herself. She didn't take herself totally seriously and she told funny stories about herself. Like this one about the train:

Absent-mindedly, one day Edna had walked "smack-dab" into a train that had stopped on the tracks at Caroline and Erb Streets in Waterloo. The force of the collision had pushed almost all her teeth in. Edna joked that it was too bad that the ones that had *really* needed the push—her front "buck" teeth were unaffected by the smack.

It was a funny story because Edna herself was the "butt" of the joke. She had no vanity, and I think that was one of the reasons that people overlooked some of her faults. It was also why she had many friends. I'm glad that for a period in my life, I was one too.

Marjorie Barber
Brockville
February 2007

---

1. In later years, Marjorie Barber became the first woman elected to the Waterloo Public School Board. As the candidate who had received the most votes, she also assumed the position of Chair.

EDNA:
THE WRITER

An original writer is not one who imitates nobody, but one whom nobody can imitate.

De Chateaubriand

Edna:
The Writer

Ivan Kraemer, Edna Martin and Salome Bearinger
"The memory of Edna presenting herself at our door remains so clear. She was not the kind of person that people forgot easily!"

June Callwood
"For all its tranquility, it also seemed like the middle of nowhere!"

Douglas Gibson
"I arrived at her side to lend some assistance, just as the last of our lunch was sliding vertically down between the oven racks."

Dr. Paul Tiessen
"...where she looks back on her early years, and confides that she felt 'in terror' of being discovered as someone hiding a secret Mennonite identity."

Ivan Kraemer, Edna Martin
and Salome Bearinger

Edna was in demand after **Maclean's Magazine** *published "Duelists of the Deep," her Cape Breton swordfish expedition, in 1948.[1] In a 1999 interview with this author, she recalled: "**Maclean's** told me that they would take anything I wrote." What* **Maclean's** *readers wanted were real "slices of life" stories of Canadians, from coast to coast.*

Maclean's *Articles Editor Pierre Berton was more specific: "You're from Mennonite country, Edna. Write a story about the horse and buggy people."[2] Edna agreed, reluctantly. She was convinced that the only way she'd be able to produce a convincing picture of her subjects was to live with them—at least for several days. And that would be no easy task, given the Mennonites' private ways.*

Nevertheless, Edna got herself to St. Jacobs, north of Waterloo, and entered the St. Jacobs General Store. She asked the owner if he knew of a local Old Order Mennonite family who might welcome her into their home. The (no doubt) startled proprietor suggested that Daniel and Leavea (Livvy) Kraemer might take her up on her request. He gave Edna directions to their home in the hamlet of Three Bridges, just outside St. Jacobs.

The year was 1949 and the intrepid journalist was on her way. Little did she imagine what adventures lay ahead.

Answering to Edna's knock, Daniel Kraemer opened the door and listened to the stranger's unusual tale. A progressive and outgoing man of the Old Order, Daniel was intrigued by her request. He agreed to her proposal to remain a week under their roof.

Thus began a close and long friendship between Edna Staebler and the Kraemer[3] family. Only a lad of 10 when Edna came to visit in 1949, Ivan Kraemer lives with his wife Agnes in Three Bridges, just a hop, skip and jump from the family homestead. His older sister Edna, then 13, and her husband Noah Martin reside a few kilometers away. The oldest sibling, Salome Bearinger, 16 at the time, lives with her husband Cleason north of Elmira. They carry with them strong memories of that unusual visit 58 years ago.

The story which follows is a compilation of two interviews with Salome, Edna and Ivan.

The memory of Edna presenting herself at our door remains so clear. She was not the kind of person that people forgot easily! But if it had been our mother who had answered the door that day, the visit might never have happened. Mother was a reserved person, until she got to warm up to someone new. I doubt if she would have agreed to Edna's request.

But Dad was friendly, outgoing and usually up for a new experience. I think his answer has become pretty well-known: "You're welcome to stay, but I think we'll find out more about you, than you will about us." And so it was.

Blending in with the Family

It was late spring or early summer when Edna arrived. I know that because the beans sprouted when she was here. She'd help Mother and I out in the garden, in the kitchen or wherever we were.[4] But she'd also go into the barn to see what Dad was up to. In the evening, once chores were done, we'd sit and talk. Edna "made up" with all of us so easily. She was such an interesting person, and told wonderful stories of Cape Breton Island and of the sword fishing trip she'd taken. To people like us, this was so new and so exciting.

On Sunday, she attended church with us. The service was in Pennsylvania Dutch, so I'm sure she didn't understand a word, but those things never seemed to bother Edna. She was up for anything.

We kids were so curious about her life, as we hadn't had the opportunity to talk to many people outside our community. I can recall that one of the first questions we asked her was how

many children she had. She said she had 31 ½ kids! We thought
that was so funny. She joked around with us a lot, and we liked
that.

Everyone was sorry when Edna left. We'd all grown very
fond of her, and made her promise that she would visit us
again—and soon. After she was gone, the house just didn't seem
the same. The loss of a person like Edna makes a big hole.

The Story is Published

*Edna's story, "How to Live Without Wars and Wedding Rings" was
published by* Maclean's Magazine *in April, 1950.[5] It established
Edna's reputation as a full-fledged journalist, and won for her the
Canadian Women's Press Award for the best piece of journalism
written by a woman.*

She brought several copies of the magazine for us to read.
We loved it. And the people who knew that we were the ones in
the story liked it, too. But I'd guess that few in the area would
have known that the story was about us. We didn't talk much
about it.

Edna kept her promise and dropped in to visit us from
time to time. She was now traveling regularly to other parts
of Canada doing research for the stories she was writing for
Maclean's. We were always so interested in the tales she'd tell
about the places she'd been, and the people she'd met. She
usually brought pictures to show us. It was a highlight for a
family who had done little traveling outside Waterloo County.

On one visit Edna announced that she was taking a trip to
Europe. Dad, who liked to joke around, told her to "watch out
for Spaniards with knives." We all had a great laugh later when
we got a postcard from Edna from Spain, referring to Dad's
little joke.

A Cockney? In Three Bridges?

Occasionally, Edna would bring along guests who were staying
with her. One visitor was Lady Ann Tenant, a woman Edna had

met during her trip to London, England. Apparently Ann was a distant relation to the Royal family. But what Dad was really interested in was her accent. He asked her about it, and she replied that she was a "Cockney."

"What's a Cockney?" Dad asked, and Ann answered rapidly: "A person born within the sound of the Bow Bells in London." From then on, Dad just loved to tell people about what a Cockney was, and the words: "born within the sound of the Bow Bells" just rolled off his tongue.

Livvy Becomes "Bevvy"

Edna continued to come up to see Mother and Father after they sold the farm in 1951. But in the mid-60's, the visits increased. Edna was now working on her cookbook, *Food that Really Schmecks* and she was using quite a few of Mother's recipes from her "little black cookbook."[6] So they spent a lot of time talking about food. A look through *Schmecks* shows recipes like: "Bevvy's Geschtuffle (Stuffed) Steak," "Bevvy's Doughnuts" and "Bevvy's Chilly(sic) Sauce."

Another recipe, for a rolled cookie called "Rigglevakes" or "Railroad" cookies was also included. Little did Edna or Mother know what a big fuss some people would make of these cookies 20 years later.[7]

As Edna had done for her *Maclean's* story, she protected our family's privacy by using false names for us. But they were different ones than she had used there.[8]

New York Lawyers Descend

By 1981, a food war was brewing over the border. Two giants in the American food industry, Proctor & Gamble and Nabisco were doing legal battle regarding a patent for a cookie recipe—"crisp on the outside; chewy on the inside." When a similar recipe, "Riggelvake" or "Railroad" cookies had been found in a cookbook, **Food that Really Schmecks**, *by Canadian author, Edna Staebler, the culinary world*

*turned their eyes on Canada. More specifically on tiny Sunfish Lake
and Mennonite country, north of Kitchener-Waterloo.*

*Lawyers and media descended en masse to the area. And while
Edna reveled in the attention, Livvy Kraemer and Edna's other
Mennonite friends found the spotlight glaring.*

It was quite silly when we look back on the "Cookie Wars"
now. The lawyers wanted to talk to Mother, who was now
over 80, all about the cookies. I can't remember if they had her
baking cookies too, but they did have others in our community
doing it. "Rigglevakes" with butter; "Rigglevakes" with lard;
"Rigglevakes" with white sugar; "Rigglevakes" with brown
sugar; "Rigglevakes" in the freezer; or in the refrigerator, or
in the cupboards…and on and on. We all thought it was quite
funny, because most people don't even like "Rigglevake"
cookies. They're too dry!

At first, it was something different and a bit of fun. But
then it dragged on. When Edna told us that the lawyers were
thinking about having some of the women, including Mother,
testify in court, it wasn't funny anymore. Edna was unhappy
about this too. One day, when Edna, and yet another lawyer,
were paying yet another visit to Mother, Edna barked out: "I'm
surprised that you're not testing their well water, too!"

Mother reached the boiling point when one of the lawyers
told her that they wanted to take her cookbook to New York
for the trial. That was when she said: "Enough is enough! You
are not taking my cookbook anywhere." And they didn't. This
small Mennonite woman had thrown a monkey wrench in all
their plans.

And so things just fizzled out after a while. Did anything
ever come of it?[9]

Two Friends Grow Old Together
Mother and Edna were fairly close in age. Mother had been born
in 1902, and Edna, four years younger, was born in 1906. Both

of them remained independent well into their mid-90's. Only in Mother's 97th year was she not able to remain any longer in her own home. So, she came to live with Cleason and me (Salome). I think that Edna was independent also until she was 96 or 97.

We've kept a very precious photograph of Edna and Mother, taken in 2001. Edna is 95 and Mother is 99.[10] You can see by the look in Mother's eyes how she felt about Edna. She was so fond of her. As all of us were.

Occasionally we think back on Edna's friendship with our family and are amazed at her devotion to us. She could have gotten what she wanted for her *Maclean's* article and gone away after that. She didn't *have* to stay in touch with us, but she did. Keeping friends close was as natural as breathing to Edna.

But even the word "friend" really doesn't express what we thought of her. She was like a sister, a family member. She'd lived with us, had gone to church with us, and knew us for who we were. And she was the most special person we've ever known.

Ivan Kraemer, Edna Martin, Salome Bearinger
Three Bridges and Elmira
May 2007

---

1. Edna Staebler, "Duelists of the Deep," *Maclean's Magazine*, July 15, 1948, 45-48.

2. Interview with author, August 1999.

3. For the *Maclean's* article, Edna chose to give the Kraemers pseudonyms. Daniel became David; Leavea was Hannah; oldest daughter Salome was renamed Salema; daughter, Edna and son, Ivan were recast as twins, Levi and Levina.

4. It was the custom, then, with Old Order Mennonite children to leave school at age 14.

5. Edna Staebler, "How to Live Without Wars and Wedding Rings," *Maclean's Magazine*, April 1, 1950, 40-44.

6. Livvy Kraemer's "little black cookbook" can be seen in the photo section of this book.

7. Dare Foods Ltd, co-CEO Bryan Dare and lawyer Michael Manson recall the "Cookie Wars" elsewhere in this book.

8. In *Food that Really Schmecks*, "Hannah" (Leavea/Livvy) became "Bevvy"; "David" (Daniel) remained the same; "Salema" (Salome) retained her own Christian name; "Levina" (Edna) was now "Lyddy Ann," and "Levi" (Ivan) re-emerged as "Amsey."

9. Michael Manson reveals the outcome of the 6-year long cookie brou-ha-ha in his story.

10. Livvy Kraemer passed away in March 2003, at the age of 100.

June Callwood

June Callwood's path first crossed Edna's at Maclean's Magazine in the early 1950's. Both writers were regular contributors of articles for the publication. Edna was primarily known as a writer of human interest stories. June's articles tended more towards hard-hitting social justice issues.[1]

Although they were not close friends, the two occasionally found themselves at the same social event. June was a part of a loose social clique she affectionately called "the Maclean's Gang." These staffers and freelancers circled around Pierre Berton, then the magazine's Articles Editor, and Ralph Allen, its Associate Editor. As Edna's friendship with Berton grew, she was also drawn into the "Gang."

June's most vivid memory of Edna came from a singular social event that she, Edna, and mutual friend Janet Berton attended. She dates it to the late 1960's. June stated that the particulars of the day remained "unforgettable" some 40 years later.

Edna was to be the guest of honour at a luncheon given by an Old Order Mennonite woman friend.[2] She invited both Janet and I to tag along. I wasn't sure why I was included, as Edna and I were not fast friends. However, I was close to Janet; perhaps that was the connection. Or maybe Edna just thought that I'd find it interesting. I'd lived in Kitchener for a year when I was a teenager and had attended K.C.I. but I certainly had never been in the company of Old Order Mennonites before, and I'll admit that I was curious.

Janet and I came from Toronto and picked Edna up at Sunfish Lake. It was my first time at her home, and I thought it serene. I was charmed by the peacefulness there, beside the lake with the simple cottage set among the trees. But I must admit too that for a big-city-living gal like me, I also found it pretty remote. For all the tranquility, it seemed to me also like the "middle of nowhere."

But it was obvious that Edna was in love with her home. Before we left for the luncheon, the 3 of us walked out to the dock in front of Edna's cottage and she told me that in the summer she swam around the lake every day. I couldn't help thinking of what might be watching a swimmer's legs from down below!

We packed into my car and started off to the party. Edna told us that her friend's farm was somewhere "up country." Up and down gravel roads we went, kicking up a cloud of dust behind us; past farms with long, long laneways and by interminable fields of corn. Many of the places we passed had no hydro lines going into the homes. We were deep in Mennonite Country. And oh! Was it hot!

Finally, we arrived at the hostess' farm. I knew her name once, but it's been lost to memory. We headed up the long drive towards the house. Despite the heat of the day, the home was relatively cool, having been shut up against the heat in the morning and with some fans going. After introductions were made, and there was a bit of chit-chat, we were served.

It was obvious that the hot weather hadn't put a crimp on the hostess' cooking and baking agenda. Before us was a feast to feed a football team. Never had I seen so much food in my life—sausage, ham, potato salad, jellied salad, cabbage salad, fresh bread, home-churned butter. And then came the desserts. Oh my! Cherry, blueberry, raspberry pies; cookies and some delicious kind of pudding. I'd never tasted anything so sinful!

Quilts, quilts and more quilts!

Apart from the food, I have other particular memories of that day. For one, neither the hostess nor her 4 daughters sat down, and none of them joined us in eating. They were certainly friendly and would gladly stop to chat, but they knew their roles as cooks and servers.

My eyes had fallen on a handsome corner cupboard in the room that held a several colourful quilts. I asked the hostess about them and she took me upstairs to see more. They were gorgeous and done in such detail. She explained that it was customary in Mennonite homes for each daughter to have 10 quilts, before they married and laughed that with 4 daughters, they had a distance to go before achieving this milestone.

Thinking back on that day, my memories turn now to the guest of honour—Edna Staebler. While I may have known, at the time, the specific reason for the celebration, I don't remember now. But I do recollect how well-regarded and admired she was in this social setting. Edna was clearly enjoying the party and her role as honoured guest, but she was no *prima donna*. Open, friendly and at ease, she gave her full attention to whomever person addressed her. It was clear to see why people adored her.

We left Edna's party, stuffed and happy, and chattered all the way back to Sunfish Lake. Janet and I then turned our car eastward, back to the hustle and bustle of our city lives.

My path rarely crossed again with Edna's, until 1985. At that time, the eyes of the food world had turned to Sunfish Lake, when Edna, unwittingly, had become involved in a legal battle between food giants Nabisco and Proctor & Gamble over cookies. I wrote an article for *The Globe and Mail* about the culinary tiff, calling them the "Cookie Wars."[3]

If my memory serves me right, I think Edna was annoyed at me about it, for some reason.[4]

In the story, I had observed that while no blood had ever been spilled in the "Cookie Wars," the other traditional elements of human warfare were manifest: the combat was expensive; the battle was fundamentally silly; it concerned itself with money, vanity and power; and the people who declared war weren't the ones doing the fighting. Their lawyers were."

But the details of that tale belong to another.

June Callwood
Toronto
November 2006

1. After a four-year battle with cancer, June Callwood passed away on April 14, 2007.

2. Edna's friend, Eva Bauman, the hostess of Edna's luncheon has quite different memories of the party and its timing. They are recounted in Eva's story, elsewhere in this book.

3. June Callwood, "Companies Wait to see how Legal Cookies Crumble," *Globe & Mail*, December 11, 1985.

4. Edna resented June Callwood's identification of her in the article as "a pleasant Canadian woman who writes cookbooks." *Must Write: Edna Staebler's Diaries.* ed. Christl Verdyn (Waterloo, Wilfrid Laurier Press, 2005), p. 229.

Douglas Gibson

By 1968 Edna's star was shining brightly. Food that Really
Schmecks *was a Canadian best-seller and cooks across the country
were clambering for more* Schmecks. *But Edna had another project
she wished to see first on bookstore shelves. For close to a quarter-
century, she had been working on her* Cape Breton Harbour *book,
and with the success of* Schmecks, *publishers were finally showing an
interest in it. In 1972, McClelland and Stewart published her labour
of love.*

*It was around this time that Edna and Douglas Gibson met.
Doug was, at the time, Publisher at McMillan of Canada.*

I met Edna at a Toronto party. Of course, I knew who she was.
This was after *Schmecks* and *Cape Breton Harbour* had been
published. But even if I hadn't recognized her, she still would
have stood out. Edna was 70-ish—definitely an older woman
at a gathering of mostly younger folk. And she was clearly out
of her element; Edna was certainly no "city slicker," as most of
the others were. She left early, as I did—I'm a small town boy
myself.

Our paths didn't cross again until 1986, when I'd moved
over from McMillan to McClelland and Stewart—some time
after M&S had published Edna's *More Food that Really Schmecks*.
By this time, Edna was working on the third of the *Schmecks*
series and we'd decided to have a company-wide contest to
name the book. The prize would be a visit to Sunfish Lake for
the winner and a guest to have "lunch with Edna." I suggested
Schmecks Appeal and won. My guest at the luncheon would be
my mother, who was visiting me at the time from Scotland. She
was about Edna's age—in her 80's, and I knew they'd hit it off.

We arrived at Sunfish at the appointed time and were
welcomed by a heavenly aroma coming out of Edna's kitchen.
She was cooking Quiche Lorraine and hoped we would like
it. We chatted for awhile and then Edna excused herself to the

kitchen. Amidst a lot of rattling and slamming came an un-grandmotherly "Oh shit! I've dropped the quiche!" I arrived at her side to lend some assistance, just as the last of our lunch was sliding vertically down between the oven racks.

We made the decision to work in tandem to salvage what we could of the egg-y mess. While I held the pie plate, Edna swooped what she could back into it. No matter, Edna handled this kind of annoyance with her usual aplomb and good humour. It was surely an "Edna moment." And I remember the lunch as being delicious, even if it lacked Ritz Hotel presentation. We ate it all up!

Shenanigans in the Board Room

Schmecks Appeal was a great hit just as the preceding *Schmecks* and *More Schmecks* had been. Then Edna came up with the idea to organize many of the recipes from the previous books into different categories—and present them in a series of slimmer books. So one volume might be "Cakes and Cookies;" another "Yeast Breads:" another "Casseroles," and so on.

She also suggested that McGraw-Hill Ryerson, who had originally published *Food that Really Schmecks* work together with M&S to put out the new series. It would be called *The Schmecks Appeal Cookbook Series*. This seemed like a good idea to both publishers and so it would be. The "fireworks" started with the first joint meeting (Edna present, of course) where the terms of her contract were to be discussed.

Edna's philosophy was clearly "smile sweetly and ask for the moon." I was flabbergasted with some of her demands—more advance money, a bigger slice of the revenue from the sales of the books, more books printed, and so on. Edna was way out of line, but she seemed to have McGraw-Hill Ryerson eating out of her hand!

When I'd hold firm to what I felt was reasonable, she'd counter with—smiling sweetly, of course: "Well, McGraw-Hill doesn't seem to have a problem with this, Doug. Why do you?"

G-r-r-r! Demanding? You bet your life! Edna was very aware of how to use that little old lady smile and charm to camouflage a tough business woman who knew what she wanted, and was darned determined to get it.

One didn't have to be overly perceptive to guess that in the past, she'd probably used the "innocent abroad" persona to get what she wanted, especially from men. And she could still do it—maybe even better than when she was a young thing. At age 80, Edna was one apple-cheeked grandmotherly negotiator from hell!

As negotiations dragged on, it was painfully obvious that I was being painted, and very skillfully too, as the "bad guy." McGraw-Hill Ryerson was clearly, the "good guy." But in the end, we compromised, and Edna got a very good book deal— but not quite as good as she wanted.

Outside the boardroom Edna and I remained as we had been for years—great friends and admirers of each other. This gave me solace for any upcoming Edna skirmishes.

Edna at the Podium

In 1997, Edna had been invited to give the Margaret Laurence Memorial Lecture at the annual meeting of the Writers' Union Conference in Kingston. It was a great honour for her, and as her publisher I wanted to be there to show my support.

So I blasted out of work early to make the drive from Toronto to Kingston, braving the Friday night rush hour traffic. I arrived at the conference just as Edna was beginning her speech and slipped into the back row. Speaking off the cuff, and without visible notes, as she usually speaks, Edna begins a perspective of her career. Abruptly, she stops, mid- sentence, to announce: "I see that my publisher Doug Gibson has just arrived. And Doug, I want to say right here and now that I was really disappointed in the poor publicity that McClelland and Stewart did for my last book."

Everyone in the auditorium turns around in their respective

seats, noticeably in great amusement at my discomfort. I have turned beet red and am attempting to slide further down in my back-row seat. "She's beating me up again," I mutter to myself, smiling grimly through my teeth. Missing nary a beat, Edna sails on to the next item on her agenda, *Schmecks Appeal*. "Oh brother," I groan to myself, "here it comes again." Edna doesn't disappoint.

"And Doug Gibson, are you still there in the back row? I want to tell you what a terrible job M &S did in marketing *Schmecks Appeal*... and Edna glides on. Any shred of dignity that I might have had at this point has disappeared. As the crowd shrieks with delight, I cover my head with my two hands and do my best to join my tattered dignity on the auditorium floor.

After Edna's talk concludes, we meet as the old friends we are, and I congratulate her on the success of her address. I note to her as well how glad I am to have braved construction madness and traffic mayhem on the 401 to have been able to catch all her speech. Smiling sweetly, she tells me she loves me and gives me a hug. Edna! How could you not love that gal!

Douglas Gibson
Toronto
June 2007

Dr. Paul Tiessen

As a new member of Wilfrid Laurier University's faculty in the 1970's, Dr. Paul Tiessen, Professor of English and Film Studies had participated in several of the "cultural tours" organized by his (then) colleague Dr. Gerry Noonan. Paul believes that it was on one of these Noonan-inspired adventures that his path first crossed with Edna Staebler's.

Over the subsequent years, Paul and his wife Hilde Froese Tiessen, a faculty member at Conrad Grebel College at the University of Waterloo, would occasionally find themselves in the same social company with Edna. Their friendship grew. The Tiessens shared much in common with her, not the least of which was a Mennonite heritage.

Paul recalls his surprise on learning of the young Edna's feelings towards her Mennonite roots.

The publication of Edna's diaries[1] uncovered her dread, her anxiety, during the 1920's and 1930's of family connections to the Mennonite world. This seemed at odds with the admiration and affection for Mennonites shown in her *Maclean's* articles in the early 1950's, and later in her cookbooks.

I read with interest her diary entry of March 6, 1975 where she looks back on her early years and confides that she felt "in terror" of being discovered as someone hiding a secret Mennonite identity. She says:

"As I grew older, I was ashamed of my parents. They weren't in society; didn't dance or play golf. I corrected their grammar. They came of local stock. Daddy's people were Mennonite pioneers. I didn't want my friends to know that. During the First World War, I suspected that they were pro-German and I was scared of that too. I was thoroughly British in all my sentiments.

...I suppose I was always afraid I'd be found out, that
my background would not be acceptable to my friends,
my WASP friends and they'd drop me, ridicule me....
I'd heard my WASP friends deriding people who were
Mennonite."[2]

"The Departure"

Her anxiety notwithstanding, Edna went on to write a one-
act play for a Kitchener-Waterloo Little Theatre competition in
the late 1930's, when she was about 30 years old. Called "The
Departure,"[3] the play is about the anguish felt by a Mennonite
mother at the breaking up of her family; at the loss of her 22-
year old son...who wishes to make a living, not on the family
farm, but with his uncle in the city. He wants to exchange his
black hat for a fashionable light grey fedora. His mother feels
only grief at the dissolution of her family:

"Ach why oh why did I leave him to in the city
for his holidays last winter? Ever since then he has
had these dumm (sic) notions to leave the farm."[4]

Although Edna seems ambivalent about how things end
for the family in the play, we feel throughout something of the
full force of "home" that she links to Mennonite country life.

Edna wrote "The Departure" about people who were distant
from her during the 1930's—indeed, quite exotic. At that time,
she knew Mennonites "only from seeing them at the market,"
as Veronica Ross points out in her Staebler biography.[5] Yet,
Edna invented such a strong interpretation of the Mennonite
home, one that she might not have found in lives such as her
own. Edna herself, like her friends in town, had, long ago left
home, gone off eagerly to school in Toronto, expressed a desire
to travel, perhaps even to avoid marriage, and certainly in her
case, the boredom of conventional family life.

So, it is not to the families that she knew best that she turned
to for her poignant treatment of this topic in the play. Rather

she projects strong definitions about family onto her Mennonite subjects. This anticipates her treatment of Mennonites for which she would become best known in *Food that Really Schmecks*, with its strong evocation of Mennonite family life. But by then, she had come to know this first hand.

Always Last to Leave
I think back also to a visit several years ago when Edna was in her mid-90's. Hilde and I arrived at Sunfish Lake to take her into a dinner party at Conrad Grebel College at the University of Waterloo, where she was to be guest speaker. She spoke with charm and wit about her life and work, easily embracing and delighting the audience that spanned a few generations.

Later, many members of the audience stayed on to chat with her. Despite her advanced age, she remained bright and engaged, right to the last guest. Edna's curiosity about and interest in many topics was infinite and she seemed always wanting to be the last to leave the party, refusing to miss a thing. Hildi and I finally convinced her it was time to go home and she reluctantly agreed.

We drove back to her idyllic cottage at Sunfish Lake, where, with the moon glistening off the snow, Edna invited us in for some tea.

Dr. Paul Tiessen
Waterloo
November 2006

1. *Must Write: Edna Staebler's Diaries*, ed. Christl Verduyn (Waterloo: Wilfrid Laurier Press, 2005), pp. 181-182.
2. Ibid, p.25.
3. Edna Staebler's unpublished play "The Departure" is housed in the Edna Staebler Collection, University of Guelph Library
4. The quote from "The Departure" is used with permission of the University of Guelph's Library Special Collections, p.6.
5. Veronica Ross, *Edna Staebler: A Life: To Experience Wonder* (Toronto: Dundurn Press, 2003), pp. 66-68.

Edna:
the Cook, and Star of
"The Cookie Wars"

*"I never see any home cooking.
All I get is fancy stuff."*

Prince Philip, Duke of Edinburgh.

Edna:
The Cook and Star of
the "Cookie Wars"

Eva Bauman
"I'm sure I speak for the others when I say that I was glad when they ('Cookie Wars' lawyers) all went away and left us to our normal lives."

Janet Berton
"I observed that men were particularly charmed by Edna…because she made them feel like what they said was important."

Michael Manson
"No Edna would not suffer fools…She had a subtle, but direct way of letting the person know when the conversation was over."

Bryan Dare
"To Edna, who was now in her 80's the brou-ah-ha (the "Cookie Wars") was a ripe opportunity to have some fun."

Eva Bauman

A friend of Edna's from the time she was a young woman still living on her parents' farm, Eva's memories of their friendship are recalled in the section " Edna: the Friend." However Eva (and her late sister Hannah) also played significant roles in both the writing of Edna's second cookbook More Food that Really Schmecks, *and the infamous "Cookie Wars." Her recollections of these memorable times in the kitchen with Edna are presented here.*

Edna's *Food that Really Schmecks* cookbook had been a great success. And she'd been asked by her publishers to do another, *More Food that Really Schmecks.* Edna visited me one day and asked if perhaps Hannah and I could help her with the second volume. We were both eager to do it. Being with Edna was always so much fun.

On any given day, Edna would arrive with her notebook; I'd put the tea kettle on and the 3 of us would sit down at the kitchen table to work. I say work, but it was a lot of just chatting too. We loved her stories about the places she'd been, and the people she'd met. Being Old Order Mennonite didn't mean we couldn't thrill to the adventures that other people had!

We worked mostly from handwritten recipe books; one was mine and one had been passed down to me by my mother. I'd dare say that pretty well every Mennonite woman has a "little black recipe book." Both had oodles of recipes—lots of cakes, cookies, and other sweets.

Sticky Buns and Long Johns

Over several visits, Edna picked quite a few favourites, like "Sticky Buns" and "Long Johns,"—cream-filled, deep-fried buns. People love them. Edna tended to avoid recipes that had ingredients like a "cup of cream," a "pound of butter," or "6 eggs." She knew that most city cooks wouldn't have these staples in the same quantity that we Mennonite farmers had.

Hannah and I also had to point out to her that some recipes might not list the quantity of ingredients. Like flour or sugar. When I make cookies, I don't measure the flour. I just put enough in to make the cookies "right."[1] Some ingredients aren't even listed. Like sugar or salt. Put enough of them in so that you like the taste! No need to measure.

So we'd have to suggest ingredients and amount to Edna; then she'd go home and test them in her own kitchen. Once? Maybe more? I know some were flops[1] so she had to do them again and again, getting them right. Poor Edna! She had all the work; we had the fun! Even still, there were errors in the first printing of the book. The recipe for "Backwoods Pie" didn't have the flour listed to thicken the fruit. I wonder how many cooks had a very runny pie without this!

Once, Edna came up looking for "props" that would be used on the covers of the later *Schmecks* books. She borrowed some of my crockery, a rolling pin and a few dishes. Of course, whenever I take out these books, I remember these days, sitting around the kitchen table, drinking tea and chatting about food and recipes and lots more. Oh, those are warm and wonderful memories.

The Cookie Fuss

But not all my cooking memories are pleasant. One of the recipes that had been used in the first *Food that Really Schmecks* book was for "Riggelvake" (Railroad) cookies. This was the recipe that caused all the upset and the lawsuits.

Even though the recipe hadn't come from us—it had come from Livvy Kraemer's recipe book,[2] we were drawn into it. Hannah and I, and other Mennonite women from the community were paid many calls from lawyers on both sides of the argument. They wanted us to bake the cookies, using various ingredients, various methods and various cooking times. Then the lawyers would return to pick the cookies up, and take them away somewhere to be analyzed.[3]

It was fun and exciting for awhile, but then it became tedious. Too much cookie time! It took us away from our usual work and routine. Edna, as always, was very sensitive to our feelings and told the lawyers that they were taking too much of our time. I'm not sure how much good it did. After all these were big city lawyers working for the cookie companies. I'm not sure how much they really cared or understood our feelings.

I'm sure I'm speaking for the others when I say that I was glad when they all went away and left us to our normal lives.

Eva Bauman
Heidelberg
April 2007

------

1. Win Shantz has a humorous anecdote about Edna cooking "the Mennonite way," elsewhere in this book.

2. The story of Livvy Kraemer and her "little black recipe book" are told by Livvy's children, Salome Edna and Ivan, in the section on "Edna: the Writer" in this book.

3. Lawyer Michael Manson, one of the lawyers involved in the "Cookie Wars" litigation provides more details of the "goings on" later in this section.

Janet Berton

Edna's relationship with Pierre Berton began as a business one. In the late 1940's, Berton was the Articles Editor at **Maclean's Magazine,** *and Edna had begun to write human interest stories of "ordinary" Canadians for the magazine. Over the years, Pierre and Edna's working relationship grew into a deep friendship—one that was sustained for 55 years, until Berton's death in November 2004.*

Berton's wife Janet enjoyed Edna's company as well and the two women became close. Like Edna, she had published a cookbook, (co-written with Pierre in 1967) called **The Centennial Food Guide: A Century of Good Eating.** *Janet also contributed a regular food column to the* **Region of York Magazine.**

It is courtesy of this food connection that the two women took a memorable holiday in 1991.

Although neither Edna nor I considered ourselves real "foodies," we had both written cookbooks and we both loved food. So when an invitation came from the Food Writers' of America to join a group of other writers on a "food cruise," through the Panama Canal, we were both game. The idea behind the cruise was that after we returned home from this fabulous eating trip, we'd write about it in our newspapers, magazines, and cookbooks. Good publicity for them; fun for us.

Our ship would make stops at Puerto Vallarta, Acapulco and Costa Rica; then, it would pass through the Panama Canal before landing at Fort Lauderdale. It would be 10 days of food, fun and sun.

Now, anyone who's been on a cruise knows how fabulous and plentiful the food is. But we food writers were treated to meals a cut above the regular passengers on the ship. We ate with the captain each evening, and, on occasion, with the President of the Viking Line. The ship's top chefs would invariably talk to us about the food that was served. All this for the purpose of promoting the Viking Line.

One day while we were at sea, we were taken on a food tour of the various floors of the boat. On one floor, all the meat was stored; on another, the vegetables; another, the desserts, and so on. I recall being shown a locked box. Inside was the ship's supply of caviar. Nobody but the head chef got to open that one!

But still more food! At the various ports of call, our group disembarked and we were shuttled by luxury coach to top-of-the-line restaurants. There we were fêted again. After the meal, the restaurant's chefs talked to us as one cook to another, and we were given recipes for the delicacies that we'd been served. It was quite the food fantasy!

Given the close quarters on a cruise boat, even good friends can have the occasional spat or two. But with Edna, it was smooth sailing all the way. Each morning while I was still trying to sleep off the rich food of the night before, Edna would be up at the crack of dawn. She'd usually start the day with a brisk morning swim in the ship's pool, followed by some walking exercise. Edna was 85 at the time, so her discipline and dedication was even more admirable.

I have so many delightful memories of our holiday, but my fondest recollections are saved for Edna herself. Being with her over a period of time (something I'd never experienced before), made me realize what a "people magnet" she was. No matter their age or background, everyone just fell in love with her. Of course, she was interesting and funny and outgoing. Lots of folk are. But people don't gravitate to them to the extent that they swarmed around Edna. I think this happened because when you talked to her, she gave you her full attention. *You* were the only person in the room at that time. People just wanted to be around her.

I also observed that men were particularly charmed by Edna. Not because she was rich or beautiful or alluring, but because she made them feel that what they said was important. I was there when the Head Chef of the ship asked her out for a drink. She was at least 40 years older than him, and if my memory serves me well, Edna readily accepted!

After our holiday, we returned home several pounds heavier, but in fine spirits. We vowed to do it again. Unfortunately, the plan was never realized. But I'll always carry with me fond memories of cruising with Edna.

Janet Berton
Toronto
November 2006

Michael Manson

Now living in British Columbia, practicing law with the firm of Smart
& Biggar, and lecturing law students at the University of Victoria,
Michael Manson can trace his acquaintance with Edna to 1985. He was
then a young Ottawa lawyer representing Nabisco Foods. Nabisco had
become embroiled in a patent litigation with another giant of the food
industry, Proctor & Gamble. Cookies were the point of disagreement
between these two food heavy-weights.

The battle would, in time, become known as "The Cookie
Wars,"[1] and would involve Edna Staebler, as well as several of her
Old Order Mennonite friends. Michael looks back at these "never to
be forgotten" days.

My journey with Edna began some time after the "Cookie
Wars" had begun in 1984. The lawsuit was a trans-Atlantic one,
as litigation had commenced in Canada, the United States, and
opposition proceedings in Europe were before the European
Patent Office. The suit saw Proctor & Gamble as Plaintiff, and
Nabisco Brands, Frito Lay and Keebler as the Defendants.

The nature of the litigation concerned who would dominate
the cookie market in North America. Proctor & Gamble had,
prior to this time, not been involved in the cookie business,
but had decided to get into what was a lucrative market. They
employed a patent to carve a niche within that market as an
entry point, so as to be able to compete with the big 3 players in
North America—the Defendants in the said action.

Crisp on the Outside; Chewy on the Inside
The details of the litigation were as follows: Proctor & Gamble
(P&G) had developed a two-sugar, two-dough cookie. This
was supposed to approximate the "Tollhouse" cookie, which,
when baked, came out both crisp and chewy-fresh. P&G's
patent recipe involved manipulation of sugars in the cookie's

two doughs. This made the outer dough crisp (due to the use of sucrose—white sugar). The inner dough used a "humectant" sugar that absorbed water more readily and therefore remained moist and chewy. When Nabisco began making a similar cookie, the "Cookie Wars" began. P&G sued for infringement of their copyright.

The claims of the P&G patent not only included "enrobed dough" (an inner dough being enveloped in an outer one) but also a pinwheel cookie. The latter variety saw one dough being intertwined with the other dough, again to give a crisp and chewy texture.

In patent litigation, one of the ways a Defendant tries to win a case is to invalidate the claims of a patent. This is accomplished in two ways: first, by showing that the alleged invention was known *prior* to the patent application being filed. As well, the Defendant can also deny that they infringed the claims of the patent; in other words, they have not used the invention as claimed.

The Mennonite "Rigglevakes"
In this case, the Defendant (Nabisco Foods) needed to find whatever references they could to show that the alleged P&G cookie recipe was not new, or was obvious (being known from prior cookie recipes made public in the past). A key reference that came out of a worldwide search for the origins of the cookie ended up pointing to it coming from an Old Order Mennonite recipe known as "Rigglevake Kucha" or Railroad Cookies. And this is where Edna Staebler came in.

The "Rigglevake" recipe had been published in Edna's cookbook *Food that Really Schmecks*. It had, in turn, been borrowed from the cookbook of Edna's Mennonite friend, "Bevvy Martin."[2]

Interestingly, in an attempt to find a reference that would knock P&G's claim out, a search for "prior art" (earlier and other references to the "Rigglevake" cookie) had been undertaken through the Library of Congress in Washington, D.C. It was here that the reference was found in Edna Staebler's cookbook. Imagine finding this not in Canada, nor Kitchener-Waterloo, nor St. Jacobs, nor Elmira, nor Sunfish Lake, but in the capital of the United States!

So by default, Edna became embroiled in the "Cookie Wars." But she became an even bigger celebrity when an article was published in *Saturday Night Magazine*. The article regaled readers about the visits of lawyers from both sides of the confrontation to Sunfish Lake—both trying to prove their case for or against the recipe being relevant. In the background, too, was the interplay with Edna's Old Order Mennonite friends, who had no desire to be involved in the litigation.

The Cast of Characters

I was one of the lawyers hired by Nabisco to invalidate P&G's patent, and I soon found my way to Edna's door. From my first visit with her, we "clicked," and a friendship grew up. But Edna was an equal opportunity resource. She enjoyed the attention from Proctor & Gamble's lawyers too.

Don Sim, a Toronto lawyer, representing P&G was a particular favourite of hers. Don's intellect and charm dazzled her, as well as his girth and size. Before the litigation was settled in 1989, Don passed away suddenly. Edna grieved his loss, and spoke fondly of him on any occasion that his name arose.

Having said that, she was not as complimentary about some of the junior lawyers who worked with Sim on the case. If there was a lack of sincerity or integrity in a person, Edna was quick to pick it up and point it out. When people approached her, trying to elicit information or ply on her Mennonite connections, she was sceptical, and would quickly "clam up." She could spot "users," immediately—those whose only goal was to obtain information for their stories, when in fact they had little interest in the Mennonite community or in Edna.

Things Become "Ugly"

While most of the times that Edna and I shared during the "Cookie Wars" were memorable, for all the right reasons, there were a number of occasions where proceedings were not pleasant. During the research phase of the investigations, P&G had collected samples of "Rigglevake" Cookies from some of Edna's Mennonite friends. Towards the end of the litigation, it became necessary to try to get statutory declarations from them, regarding what they had done during the various bakings. This was needed, as there had been an alleged fraud on the U.S. patent office.

P&G had failed to disclose that they had tried to have the Mennonite cooks "manipulate" the "Rigglevake" recipe, so that it would not yield a crisp and chewy cookie. The allegation was that if, in fact, the cookies were baked properly, both crisp and chewy cookies would result. This would be a legitimate reference to invalidate some of the claims in the P&G patent.

If, in fact, this manipulation had occurred, and could be proven in Court, then there could be a serious attack on at least some of the claims of the United States patent. This would be extremely important to the Defendants' case.

As a result, I was asked to visit with several of the Old Order Mennonite cooks who had baked for Edna and for P&G's lawyers. During these visits, I was informed that, indeed, this manipulation had occurred. It was then necessary for me to obtain statutory declarations (sworn statements) from them. These would then be used in the United States litigation.

This action caused P&G to whirl into counter-action. They sent lawyers themselves to attempt to extract statutory declarations that cast doubt upon those which I had obtained. Some of the statements the Mennonites had made to P&G surprised me, as they were at odds with what I had heard. When this became clear, I was instructed to go back once again, this time with Edna, to try and clarify what had happened.

No Fun Anymore

The involvement of Edna's Mennonite friends distressed her. What had begun as fun for all, had now turned ugly. At the outset of the case, she had been assured that her Old Order friends would not be dragged into the fray, nor would they be compromised. This was not the case. She felt betrayed by all the lawyers—including me. I felt equally badly; however, I was just doing my job, and that was to make sure that the statements I had gathered were an accurate reflection of what had happened.

And so, I imposed upon Edna to take me to meet with the ladies one more time.

During this meeting, the Mennonites indicated they *had* been pressured and coerced into making statements with which they were not comfortable. With this turn of events, further declarations were necessary to try and clarify the situation. The whole exercise was distasteful, and strained our relationship with the Old Order Mennonites. It was not a situation that I would ever want to do again.

New York! New York!

Once all investigations in "Mennonite Country" had been concluded, the action switched to a New York court of law. And, of course, Edna was brought to "the Big Apple" too! She and her niece, Barbie, were wined and dined by New York lawyers, representing both sides of the battle. Their accommodation? At the Waldorf-Astoria—one of the most spectacular suites that I have ever seen. Touring around Manhattan? By a private stretch limo! I usually accompanied them and we attended Broadway plays, and ate at places of fine dining.

The end finally came to the "Cookie Wars" in 1989. The defendants (Nabisco, Frito Lay and Keebler) paid P&G $120 million as a settlement. This was the biggest dollar settlement for a patent litigation, at that time. However, P&G's entry into the cookie market was completely unsuccessful. They ultimately closed operations on this front on both sides of the border. So who really won?

Edna is Front and Centre

Over the 5 years that the "Cookie War" battles had raged, Edna was front and centre. And for the most part (the involvement of her Mennonite friends excepting), she loved it! Edna had been approached to write a book about the goings-on of the cookie world. Film types had also proposed a movie. After some consideration, she gave the rights to several media representatives to begin work.

But most failed to deliver, in a timely fashion. Edna had some harsh comments about broken promises. She expected as much of other people as she did of herself, and that was no small order for anyone who was involved with Edna.

One venture that did come to fruition was a play based on the "Cookie War" drama. Written by Kathleen McDonnell, it had its dramatic debut in 1988 at the Blyth Festival, in Blyth, Ontario, northwest of Stratford. For the opening night ceremonies, lawyers from Canada and the United States, and from both sides of the dispute were in attendance. They gathered at Edna's home to pick up the guest of honour. Then the party set out for the journey to Blyth, travelling in two stretch limousines.

Many in the audience recognised Edna, but must have wondered who all the "suits" were sitting with her! It would be an understatement to say that she revelled in every moment of the attention being paid to her. Before the play, at intermission and after, she was surrounded by autograph seekers. When we returned to our cars, a happy group set off eastward. On the way home, we stopped the limos, pulled to the side of the road and popped some champagne to celebrate the events of the day.

Fun and Fellowship at Sunfish

What had started as a professional relationship between Edna and me ultimately became a warm friendship. Whenever I could,

I visited Edna at Sunfish Lake—sometimes alone, sometimes accompanied by my wife, Joanne. No matter the season or occasion of my visit, I'd greet Edna with a pink or red azalea. This delighted her, and she came to expect it from me on my visits.

In the summer months, Edna always reminded me to bring a bathing suit for a swim in the lake. On occasion, lawyers from New York would join me for a dip. I recall particularly a young, good-looking lawyer named Dan Burke. I soon learned that Edna had an eye for the young men in her life. While she was never one to talk about her own looks, she certainly did notice whether a person was appealing or not. After our dip we'd relax on the porch, which overlooked the lake. It was such an idyllic and enjoyable time.

Winter at Sunfish Lake offered a different type of diversion: birds at the window. How could the visitor (or host) not be distracted by the colourful array at Edna's feeders. A steady procession of cardinals, blue jays and grosbeaks came in for a landing outside the living room window. Edna would chat away with me, while commenting on the visitors—all without breaking her train of thought or place in her story. One of her companion cats was usually curled up in a chair close to her. They were Edna's never-ending source of quiet companionship.

I also remember the piles of books that filled every bookcase, every wall, virtually every surface in Edna's home. The newest were usually candidates for her Creative Nonfiction Award, or were books written by author-friends. Piled on couches and chairs, they formed a kind of literary headrest in the Staebler home. Edna had read them all and would occasionally share her opinion of what she had digested. Sometimes, her comments were gracious; sometimes not. Edna was very direct in her criticism of what she regarded as talent, or not.

Out on a "Date"
From time to time, I'd take the role of Edna's escort to functions. I was honoured to accompany her to various public events,

including the Culinary Institute of Canada's inaugural "Edna Award" ceremony. It was here that she was honoured by having the "Lifetime Achievement Award" named after her. In accepting the "Edna Award," she addressed the crowd without a note in front of her. And, with her usual humour and approachable manner, she spent the next 45 minutes regaling the audience with stories that had them laughing one minute, almost in tears the next. This is a quality that few seem to have. Edna was one of those rare people and had the undeniable gift for making the ordinary extraordinary.

One of Edna's favourite eating places was Rundles, a particularly trendy, upscale restaurant in Stratford, owned by Edna's friend, Jim Morris. Edna's entrance into the restaurant was handled with a celebrity-like attention. Throughout the meal, she was always treated like a queen, by both the owner and his staff.

While Edna was not a frequent imbiber, she did love the champagne that Jim always offered to start the evening. She also enjoyed having the occasional drink and we'd often share cocktails when we went out for dinner. Other "dates" were less high-profile, but no less enjoyable. I recall a visit to a local farm to share tea and "pull cake" with some Mennonite friends.

Reflecting Back on a Great Lady
Thinking back to the Edna Staebler I knew, many descriptions come to mind. I was always impressed with how she approached all situations with good grace and humility. But, at the same time, the sparkle in her eye showed she was enjoying every minute of it. It became clear to me that in her younger days Edna must have been quite a free spirit and had enjoyed a fair amount of male attention.

It was always apparent though when Edna didn't think much of a particular person. She wasted little time or words with him or her. No, Edna would not suffer fools. She had a subtle, but direct way of letting such a person know when the conversation was over, or it was time for them to leave. I saw her use this skill a number of times, over the years.

And without becoming self-centred and self-absorbed, Edna was immensely proud of her success. She enjoyed too the popularity that had come as a result of her articles and cookbooks. She held dear her friendships with other luminaries in the Canadian literary world. Edna delighted in telling tales of her encounters with Pierre Berton and his wife Janet, Farley Mowat, June Callwood, and many other distinguished Canadians. While she appeared outwardly humble about her popularity, it still pleased her immensely to have a full entertainment agenda and to be the focus of the public's attention.

Perhaps one of the most endearing and lasting qualities I'll remember about Edna is the loyalty she showed to her friends. Notwithstanding the many stresses and strains that signalled the different points of her life, she always exuded a warmth, caring and joy for every moment of every day. She returned to those who called her "friend," a full measure of love and affection.

And so my thoughts of Edna come to a close. I'm grateful for the opportunity I had to meet her and to share with her in such a unique time of her life. More importantly, I am thankful that she became a dear friend.

Michael Manson
Vancouver
June 2007

---

1. Writer June Callwood penned this phrase in an article that she wrote for the *Globe & Mail* called "Companies Wait to see how Legal Cookie Crumbles," (December 11 1985). June refers to it in her story.

2. Out of respect for the Kraemers, in whose house Edna had lived while researching her "How to Live without Wars and Wedding Bands" article for *Maclean's Magazine,* and in *Food that Really Schmecks*, Edna had given pseudonyms to the family. "Bevvy Martin" was, in actuality, Leavea (Livvy) Kraemer.

Bryan Dare

Dare Foods co-CEO Bryan Dare's introduction to Edna came as a result of a charity auction. His parents had successfully bid on a "Tea and Muffins with Edna Staebler" prize and he accompanied them to Sunfish Lake for the outing. Some years later, when Bryan was in Edna's neighbourhood, he "got up the courage" to knock on her door to pay a repeat call. He remembers his reception as "warm and welcoming," and he made Edna a pledge to visit more often. This opportunity presented itself shortly.

In the mid-1980's, Edna had been drawn into a protracted dispute between food giants Nabisco and Proctor & Gamble over ownership of a cookie recipe. An approximation of the disputed recipe had appeared 20 years earlier as "Rigglevakes" in Edna's Food That Really Schmecks. *Now lawyers for the two American companies descended on Sunfish Lake to wine and dine Edna. Each side hoped to win her favour. The media soon picked up the story and Sunfish Lake was overrun with journalists and television reporters.*

It was at this point that Bryan Dare called on Edna.

Scarcely a day went by without some mention of the goings-on of the so-called "Cookie Wars" on television or in the newspaper. Often, it appeared that somehow Edna was in the middle of it. Knowing the cookie business from the inside, I wondered if I could be of any help to her. So I invited myself out to Sunfish Lake for a visit.

I found out that my instincts were correct. Edna understood few of the intricacies of the legal battle going on around her. I recall her laughing, saying: "I just entertain the lawyers when they show up." Nor did she *want* to know much about the issues. To Edna, who was now in her 80's, the brou-ha-ha was a ripe opportunity to have some fun.

And what a lot of fun she was having! There were television and newspaper reporters wanting interviews, to say nothing of nice young lawyers paying their respects, bringing her flowers and wining and dining her at fancy Stratford restaurants. Oh yes, Edna was just loving it! But I don't want to give the impression that Edna was a publicity seeker or an opportunist. It wasn't like that at all. Edna just liked to enjoy herself, and she was. All courtesy of a cookie recipe!

So when the lawyers wanted her to come to New York to testify in the courts, she was up for that experience too. Why not? Stretch limousines, staying at a fancy hotel and eating at the best restaurants. For Edna it was a matter of seizing the moment—*carpe diem*. I think she was almost disappointed when the whole thing was finally resolved.

In retrospect, I think that it was seeing Edna's *joie de vivre* that drew so many people—including myself into her world. For her, the luxuries of life were so much less important than the experiences surrounding them.

And this was what I found most attractive about Edna; that ability to turn almost anything into something that brought herself, and other people, joy. And to the end of her life, this never wavered.

Bryan Dare
Kitchener
December 2006.

Edna:
The Celebrity

The best fame is a writer's fame:
it's enough to get a table in a good
restaurant, but not enough that you get
interrupted when you eat.

Fran Lebowitz
The Observer

Edna: the Celebrity

Veronica Ross
"She became 'The Edna Staebler,' the positive, energetic and upbeat person so many of us knew and admired."

Peter Etril and Marilyn Snyder
"The closest I can come to describing Edna's reaction was 'startled.' 'It's way too bright!'"

Pat Zehr
"The look on Edna's face was a delight, and one I'll never forget. It said plain and clear...'Well, Wilmot you finally got it right!'"

Minas Vassiliadis
"Edna loved chatting even more than riding in limousines!"

Hilde Slezak
"*Ruby's Letters* affected me as no book had before, or has since."

Jean Wright
"My heart quickens when she approaches us again. No longer just my apple head dolly lady, she's a celebrity in my midst."

Marylu McGrath and Marilyn Berge
"I had to chuckle. Edna Staebler, world-famous cookbook author hauling stale cake out of her freezer!"

Shirley Schweitzer
"Edna took one bite of the Chelsea Bun and declared: 'These are the *best* Chelsea Buns I've ever eaten.'"

Catherine Vassiliadis

"Why would she want to miss the telephone calls and the in-person visits...for a few fleeting moments of fame on American television?"

Trustee Catherine Fife

"Fifty-eight people sent in suggestions....Forty-three of these were in honour of Edna Staebler."

Veronica Ross

Veronica Ross of Kitchener first became acquainted with Edna Staebler through their shared membership in the Writers' Union of Canada. After Veronica was selected to become Kitchener Public Library's first "Writer-in-Library" in 1996 (a position created thanks to a generous financial donation to the KPL from Edna), their paths crossed again. The friendship deepened when, in 1997, they shared a drive to Kingston where Edna was delivering the Margaret Laurence Memorial Lecture to the annual Writers' Union general meeting.[1]

I found her pleasant; not elderly in the least, with a great sense of fun. By the end of the trip, I'd learned much about Edna's long and eventful life—enough to want to know more. Little did I guess how soon my wish would be fulfilled. Sometime after that trip, Edna asked me if I'd consider writing her biography. I hesitated, momentarily, due to my involvement in other writing projects. But I soon realized that this was an invitation I must not refuse.

I Didn't Want to Leave

Over the next year, I made at least 50 weekly trips to Sunfish Lake, and recorded over 200 hours of conversation. I'd arrive for our interviews in the early afternoon, and within moments, the feeling of warmth and timelessness that surrounded Edna and Sunfish Lake enveloped me. Before I had realized it, the sun was setting, and I had to return to that "other" world. It was so difficult to say goodbye. My only consolation was that I would soon come again.

Recalling this magical time in my life, my memories are many and varied: memories of Edna, herself—her voice, her laughter, her face, her gestures— as we sat and talked; then memories of the stories she told about those she had shared her life with, and those she had loved; memories of the events that had touched, excited and challenged her.

Love and Loss

Edna was forthcoming to me about most aspects of her life, even regarding her love affairs. Only once did she request that I omit a sensitive incident, or refrain from identifying a certain person. She spoke openly too about her unhappy marriage and eventual divorce. Even though this had occurred almost 50 years before, Edna still became emotional when we discussed it. Keith was, she revealed, the "love of her life," and her marriage breakup was the hardest thing she had ever had to face in her life. I've seen pictures of her taken at this time. Her face is pinched and sad; her smile is forced. Photos do not lie, and one sees the deep hurt in Edna's heart.

But she was a strong woman—certainly stronger than the image (which she disliked) of the grandmotherly, happy homemaker, in a tidy apron, pulling cookies out of the oven. Once, she showed me a picture that hung on her bedroom wall. It's a silly picture, really, of two Victorian-era little girls, in long ringlets and looking very feminine.[2] A butterfly is flitting around their heads. The expression on their face is one of terror. These little protected girls were afraid of the butterfly! Edna said she looked at the picture when she needed a reminder to be strong; when she wanted to convince herself how silly fear is.

One Area Remains Closed

Only in regards to one aspect of her life, was Edna less than forthcoming with me. This was in *how* she learned to banish fear and negative thinking. I'm not certain whether it was a fault of mine in interviewing her; whether Edna was unwilling to talk about it, or it was her inability in articulating her feelings well on this subject. In any case, this is not an area that I discovered. However, since that time, I've developed some theories.

I don't believe that Edna *never* had negative or maudlin thoughts; what I believe is that she had learned to *re-direct* them into positive or optimistic feelings. How did she learn to achieve this? Two possibilities come to mind: One is that Edna's mentor,

Dr. John Robbins,[3] played an important role in teaching her this. Or, perhaps she'd learned it from the books that she read, or from certain people whom she had met and admired. Whatever the source, Edna had learned to banish self-destructive and hurtful feelings, and replace them with rewarding ones. It's my feeling that she was learning this skill in the early years of her marriage; certainly she employed it much later to get her through the divorce.

Becoming "The" Edna Staebler

However Edna had accomplished this almost mind-altering skill, or from whom or what she had learned it, Edna *had* learned to face those fears—those butterflies around her head— and turn around her unhappiness. And so she was able to get a joy out of life that remains elusive to so many others. She became "The Edna Staebler," the positive, energetic and upbeat person so many of us knew and admired.

In the early years at Sunfish Lake, she had needed to work hard at it. People weren't flocking to Edna's door in the 1960's and 70's, like they did in the later years of her life. In fact, she was somewhat lonely at first. But, as in so many other situations that were wanting in her life, Edna decided to turn negativity into something positive. A good example of this comes to mind.

With Christmas coming—maybe her first or second one at the lake— she decided to send out invitations to come visit her. She baked dozens of cookies and had some "Christmas Cheer" on hand. And people responded. They found that Edna was great fun, and they liked being with her.

Coming Back—Again and Again

But why did they come back, time and time again? There were two reasons: first, Edna had this incredible power or ability to focus her attention on the people who came to visit her. This was neither forced nor faked. This is who Edna was. She made her visitors feel that they were very special, unique and what they had to say was the only thing important at the moment.

Even in her cookbooks, Edna turns her attention to the reader. In the "Neil's Harbour" bread recipe in *Food that Really Schmecks*, she addresses the cook directly, regarding a concern they might have about the rising time for bread dough.

> "If you're interrupted while mixing and kneading your dough, don't worry over it: it will simply be easier to handle when you get back to it. Cover it if you're having a long-winded phone conversation."[4]

Is it any surprise that people bought Edna's cookbooks in the thousands? Reading *Schmecks* was just like talking to Edna in person!

But there was an equally important reason why people loved visiting Edna. She was able to transfer the joy that she had learned to get out of life, to the people she talked to. This is so different than what we've come to expect from most elderly people. Edna just didn't complain about her aches and pains. She had them, but she didn't obsess about them. There were just so many more enjoyable subjects to talk to about.

So people wanted to come back, and back again, to be part of the "Edna experience." By the time she was in her 80's and 90's Edna almost had more visitors than she could handle. But, of course, she never turned anyone away.

The Book is Complete

Along the way Edna didn't read or make edits to her biography. That was an understanding between us. She would read her life story for the first time once it came back from the publisher. And yes, I was worried how she'd receive it, especially how I'd presented her various relationships with men.

But she liked it, and that was a great relief. And perhaps just as important, we remained friends after the book was published. I visited her at Beechwood Manor and at Columbia Forest and saw her shortly before she passed away.

I miss Edna dearly and will always be grateful for the opportunity that she gave me. For surely, she changed my life.

Veronica Ross
Kitchener
June 2007

---

1. Elsewhere in this book, McClelland and Stewart Publisher Doug Gibson offers his humorous recollections of this event.

2. This picture is included in the gallery at the end of the book.

3. Edna and Robbins carried on a correspondence between 1945 and 1952, when Robbins passed away.

4. "Neil's Harbour White Bread" in *Food that Really Schmecks*, Toronto: The Ryerson Press, 1968, p. 138.

Peter Etril and Marilyn Snyder

Waterloo artist Peter Etril Snyder is best known for his paintings of the Old Order Mennonites living in and around the Waterloo Region. But in 1999, he was contemplating another subject synonymous to Kitchener-Waterloo—a portrait of Edna Staebler. Edna had long been a generous benefactor of the Kitchener Public Library and Peter felt that a portrait of her should hang there.

Library Administration liked the idea and suggested that he proceed. His first step was to ask the subject in question if she was agreeable. Peter and his wife Marilyn had known Edna for many years, and decided to pay a visit to Sunfish Lake.

Edna was delighted and quite flattered at what I was proposing, and both she and I were anxious to begin. So while I chatted with Edna, Marilyn took several informal photos for me to work from. My vision was not to do a formal portrait of her but one that showed a representation of the objects that made up "Edna's world"— her cats, the pictures on her walls, the many books that filled her living room and sun porch, and the assorted bric-a-brac which she treasured. This would be no sweet little old lady sitting in a rocking chair.

As an artist, I've always been sensitive to colour, and each time we had gone to Sunfish Lake, I'd been struck by the neon brightness of Edna's home. You almost had to wear sunglasses inside! There were the reds, yellows, and oranges of the various blankets and afghans she had on chairs and couches; the embroidered throw pillows, the furniture, the various paintings, not to mention the walls. I likened the colour of them to "teal on steroids!" When I looked over the photos that Marilyn had taken, I knew that these colours would play their part in the work.

The photo I chose was one where she was not looking directly into the camera. She had a quizzical look on her face and

I liked the mood it created. Over the next 12 weeks, I planned and painted (in acrylics), integrating bits and pieces of Edna's world into the central image. In a departure from the way I usually proceed with portraits, Edna wouldn't see its progress. She would view it only on completion.

The Painting Unveiled

The unveiling of the portrait at the KPL was an "event" with around 80 various dignitaries, library administration and staff, Edna-fans and members of the public in attendance. Edna sat in the front row. After a few opening remarks, the portrait was unveiled.

The closest I can come to describing Edna's reaction was "startled!" "It's *way* too bright," she cried, quite audibly. People laughed. Her comment was, for me, a real revelation. It was apparent that Edna had absolutely no conception of the colours that surrounded her daily in her world.

Edna's next comment was no more positive: "I look like a turtle!" she blurted out, (a reference to her hooded eyelids). Reserve and reticence have never been strong suits for Edna.

For my part, I was neither offended nor dejected by Edna's reaction, for she did have positive comments, as well. The likeness of her cat, sitting on her knee earned high praise.

In time, I'm told, Edna made peace with her portrait,[1] which was given a place of honour in the concourse at the Kitchener Library. Although Edna never came to love the work itself, she was proud as punch that it was done. She felt honoured too that this lasting memory of her would remain long after she was gone.

Peter Etril and Marilyn Snyder
Waterloo
April 2007

---

1. Edna later discussed the portrait with two visitors to Sunfish, Marilyn Berge and Marylu McGrath. Their recollections of this event are found elsewhere in the book.

Pat Zehr

Baden's Pat Zehr was a woman community organizations could count on when looking to raise some money. In the mid- 1990's, she had taken on the task of co-chairing fund-raising for the restoration of Castle Kilbride in Baden. A celebrity auction was one of Pat's high-profile initiatives to help the cause along. One celebrity she knew the committee must not overlook for a donation was local icon Edna Staebler.

The donations for the auction were quite impressive. They included a day at a spa, an original drawing by writer Margaret Atwood, tickets to Argo and Blue Jays games, and a gift basket of fine wines from Ed Mirvish. Edna threw in "Edibles with Edna" for 6 people, served at her cottage on Sunfish Lake. Given her reputation as a good cook, as well as a well-loved local celebrity, we were sure this prize would go for quite a bit.

And it did. Wilmot Township Mayor Lynn Myers was the high bidder and took home Edna's prize. This part was easy. Picking the 5 "lucky ducks" who would accompany Lynn to Sunfish might be harder. Who *wouldn't* want to visit Edna? As fund-raising chair, I was a "shoe-in." Others included committee member Mary Lou Jonas, who was a friend of Edna's, and another one of the Township's staff. Only 4 went—all the more muffins and Edna-chat for us!

The trip out to Sunfish was high-spirited, and Edna greeted us in a similar mood. And what can I say? The day itself was "pure Edna." She was dressed in her usual comfy sweatshirt and track pants, the house was its usual "lived in" self—books, magazines, cat memorabilia, bouquets of flowers well past their best-before date. In other words Edna put on no airs for company. You got Edna as she was, and people loved her for it.

The afternoon wore pleasantly on; then Edna suddenly remembered the reason for our get-together. "Oh! The tea and the muffins! I better get the kettle on," she announced.

She jumped up from her chair like a youngster, and bolted to the kitchen. No, Edna never moved slowly. She asked Mary Lou, who knew the house well, to go down to the freezer in the basement to get out the muffins. We looked at each other. Muffins? From cookbook icon Edna Staebler? In the *basement*? And in the *freezer*?

With Mary Lou as her kitchen helper, Edna brought in the auction prize. Before us sat a dozen or so very compact muffins. No mushroom-puffed, light as air "M-M-M-Muffins" for this get-together. I can't recall if Edna "overnuked" them in the microwave but when they reached us, they were quite cold and hard. In fact, these babies could have been used for hockey pucks! They reminded me of the specimens I'd churned out in high school "Home Ec." class.

But did anyone care? Did anyone complain? Did any one refuse another? Not on your life! Bullets or not, these were *Edna's* muffins, and here we were, in *Edna's* cottage, talking, trading stories, laughing and enjoying each other's fellowship. This was reward enough for all.

At one point Edna offered an explanation why she was such a talker. "I'm hard of hearing, you know," she offered, "so if I talk all the time and don't give anyone a chance to get a word in edgewise, I won't miss any of the conversation." We all roared.

In the blink of a moment, the afternoon had sped by and the sun was beginning to set. We said our goodbyes to Sunfish Lake, to Edna, and each other. It had been a magical day.

An Oversight Rectified

My friend, Mary Lou Jonas was a goldmine of Edna-information. She shared with me that Edna was "steamed" that her recent ordination into the Order of Canada had not been recognized in her own "backyard"—Wilmot Township. In my self-appointed role as unofficial "muckraker" in the Township[1] I passed this nugget on to Mayor Myers.

Lynn agreed that something should be done for her. After all, she was the Number One celebrity in the Township. He suggested that I draw up a budget for a party to honour Edna and he'd make sure the money was found. His idea was a formal tea to take place on the lawn of Castle Kilbride. I had grander ideas!

One night during dining out with friends, the talk around the table had turned to Edna and the "do" I was engineering. One of the other dinner guests, Minas Vassiliadis, who also knew Edna, suggested that she should arrive at the fête in grand style. He had a Rolls-Royce limousine and would be glad to play chauffeur. It was an inspired idea, and I "booked" Minas for the job right then and there.[2]

Over the next few weeks, the party just got bigger and better. It would take the form of a Garden Party, to be held on the lawn of Castle Kilbride. The date, Sunday, May 26, 1996 was hopefully late enough in the spring that we wouldn't be rained on or frozen out. I'd conscripted Edna's friend Dr. Gerry Noonan to be in charge of invitations. He'd sent out several hundred, including one to Pierre Berton and his wife Janet. Punch and refreshments would be served, and the New Hamburg Band would play.

I'd volunteered to act as MC for the celebration. After some mingling time, I'd invite anyone in attendance to say a few words. Then after these formalities, a receiving line would be formed. Everyone present was encouraged to meet and greet the guest of honour. Given Edna's considerable age—past 90—she'd be seated in a "royal" chair while the tributes were being given, and would remain there as people lined up to congratulate her.

"Edna Day" in Wilmot Township

The weather was beautiful on "Edna Day in Wilmot Township." Over 300 people showed up to pay tribute to her. Everyone was gathered and waiting when, at the appointed hour, the Rolls Royce came into view and turned in the driveway of the Castle. As the limousine approached, everyone started cheering.

When the car stopped, Minas, dressed in a tuxedo and a type of Greek fisherman's cap—he looked very "snappy"— got out to open the door for Edna, who was sitting in the back seat of the car. A drum roll sounded, and Edna stepped out to the applause. The look on her face was a delight, and one I'll never forget. It said, plain and clear for all to see, "Well, Wilmot, you *finally* got it right!"

The day was a total success. Many people wanted to speak, among them Pierre Berton and Lynn Myers. But many "ordinary folk" too had their favourite Edna stories to share. Most joined the lineup to shake Edna's hand and pass on their personal greetings. And she took time with each and everyone one who was there. Just as a real queen would have done.

I'm sure Edna slept like a log that night. I know I did.

Pat Zehr
Baden
June 2007

---

1. Pat Zehr later became Lynn Myers' Office Manager when he was elected to Parliament as the Liberal M.P. for Kitchener-Conestoga riding. She remained in this position from 1997 to 2006.
2. Pat's recollection of how Minas was "drafted" to be Edna's chauffeur differs somewhat from his own, which can be read next in this book.

Minas Vassiliadis

Retired from his role as a successful businessman, Minas Vassiliadis of Durham insists he now "does nothing" for a living. When he and his wife Cathy are not puttering around the small lake that fronts onto their rural property, or watching the array of songbirds that visit them regularly, they are pursuing their plan to see as much of the world as time allows.

But on May 26, 1996, Minas had an important job ahead of him. The owner of a 1938 Rolls Royce Wraith limousine, Minas had been conscripted by his friend Gerry Noonan to chauffeur their mutual friend Edna Staebler to a V.I.P. party. On that day, she was to be fêted at a celebration held at the historic Castle Kilbride in Baden. The party was in recognition of Edna's recent investiture into the Order of Canada.

Minas recalls this memorable day in his, and in his passenger's life.

Gerry suggested to me that Edna should arrive in great style to the party. He thought that my antique Rolls Royce would be a fitting carriage for such an esteemed person. I knew from past experience that Edna loved arriving at places "in style." I'd once driven her to Rundles in Stratford, her all-time favourite restaurant, in a vintage 1931 Bentley. She felt like royalty then so I was sure she'd be delighted at this plan.

Gerry's other bright idea appealed to me less. At the get-together, there was going to be a time for people who wanted to give their best wishes to Edna publicly, and Gerry thought I should add my two cents worth. Driving I do well; public speaking I do not. However, given the occasion and the person being honoured, I agreed to this also.

The weather was beautiful on Edna's very special day. At the appointed time, I arrived at Sunfish Lake, dressed appropriately in a black pinstriped suit, shirt, tie and my gentleman's hat as befitting an important person's chauffeur. I called for her at the house, guided her to the car and opened the rear door—just like a real chauffeur would do.

The Procession Begins
Protocol calls for the passenger to sit on the left side of the car, on the opposite side to the driver. (This car was made in England, so the driver is on the right.) Protocol also has the glass partition between the driver and passenger closed for the passenger's privacy.

But I knew Edna wouldn't like this idea one bit because then she wouldn't be able to chat with me. She loved chatting even more than riding in limousines! And from what I had heard from the door to the car, she was in her usual ebullient mood. So I kept the window down.

Edna's friend Barbara Naylor drove her car behind ours— just to make certain nothing unforeseen happened to my 1938 beauty along the way. But the trip from the Lake to Kilbride was uneventful, save for Edna giving me instructions all the way. I knew how to get there! As a joke, I raised the glass partition for a few moments. We both laughed, and I later heard her telling about it to friends.

Right at the appointed hour, we pulled up to the Castle. It was a big crowd—around 300 people waiting for "The Edna." They were cheering and the band was playing. I got out of the car and opened the door for the star to make her grand entrance. And it was quite the entrance![1]

Now for the Hard Part
My first duty was over. I tried to enjoy the party, as much as I could, knowing that later, I had to do "The Speech." I would try to accomplish it as incompetently as possible—just to punish Gerry for getting me into this! The theme I had chosen was the fittingness of driving one of the best people in the world, Edna Staebler, in the best car of the world—the Rolls Royce. I did a

bit of history of both "antiques." The crowd, and Edna seemed to like it, but I hope no one was taping it.

My duties and fun for the day were now over, and I could relax. I wouldn't be chauffeuring Edna home. She had plans to spend the evening with friends. It had been quite the day—one I will never forget and one I was honoured to share with the wonderful Edna.

Peter Wants to Know Everything

A few days after the party, I tuned in the radio to hear Edna on Peter Gzowski's Morningside program. Of course, Peter wanted to know all about Edna's investiture, and he'd heard about the big party at the Castle for her, including her arrival in the Rolls Royce. He wanted all the details of that too.

And in her wonderful Edna way, she told him and his listeners everything they wanted to hear. Peter giggled as much as she did. Peter loved Edna, as we all did. I was proud that I'd been part of her big celebration too. It's not every day a guy like me gets to be a part of history like that.

Minas Vassiliadis
Durham
February 2007

---

1. Elsewhere in the book, Pat Zehr offers her interpretation of Edna arriving at the party.

Hilde Slezak

In 1980, Hilde Slezak was a widow living in Montreal when she met her future husband, Larry, who lived in Waterloo. The pair began to date, and for the next two years, Hilde made regular trips to Waterloo to see her beau. It was on one of these visits that she fell in love with—Kitchener-Waterloo, and its most famous celebrity, Edna Staebler.

Growing up in a large city like Montreal, I was immediately attracted to the "country charm" of Waterloo. And what appealed to me the most were the Mennonites. I'd never seen an Old Order Mennonite person before I visited Waterloo, and I was mesmerized by them—their clothing, their horses and buggies, their dialect and their culture. I've always been a keen reader, so when I'd go back home to Montreal, I'd search out bookstores for anything Mennonite. I bought dozens of books and couldn't wait to get home to open them.

On one visit to K-W, Larry took me to the Kitchener Market and it was there that I first saw *Food that Really Schmecks* by someone called Edna Staebler. Even though I wasn't a great fan of cookbooks, of course I had to have it, because of the Mennonite connection. Little did I know that this book would start a "love affair" with Edna.

Schmecks fascinated me. It was nothing like any of the cookbooks that I'd ever read before. *Schmecks* also read like literature. There were interesting characters to get to know between the pages—Bevvy, her husband David, their children Amsey, Salome and Lyddy Ann. Then there were Edna's relatives who also popped up in the book—her mother, and sisters Ruby and Norm. The book even had a plot—now we'll visit the soups; later the breads; with a side trip to the pies. Edna was funny and was full of off-hand comments which made me chuckle. I read it through, cover to cover, without even turning on the oven or getting out a rolling pin!

Now this might sound a bit strange, but it was my love of all things Mennonite, and Edna Staebler that influenced my decision to move here in 1982. (Oh, I guess Larry counted a bit too!)

Not Wanting it to End

After I moved to Waterloo, I took a job at Wilfrid Laurier Press—what a perfect place for a book addict like me to work! My heart did a real pitter-pat when I heard that the Press would be publishing Edna Staebler's latest book called *Ruby's Letters.*[1] As soon as it came off the press, I bought several copies (one copy for me, and two for each of my twin sisters who were also Edna fans). I counted the minutes till I could go home, put on a pot of tea and dive into Edna's new book.

Ruby's Letters affected me as no other book had before, or has since. Before I had turned a scant few pages, I was in mourning for its eventual conclusion. It was then that I decided I would read only ONE page each day, delaying its conclusion for as long as I could. I never wavered from this plan—even though I was dying to read more, and more, and more.

And when the end did eventually come, 164 days, over 5 ½ months later, I wept like I would for the loss of a dear friend. Strangely, I have never opened the book since that time—fearing that Ruby and Edna's magic might not return for me a second time.

Just the Two of Us

Some weeks later, we heard that all of us who worked at the Wilfrid Laurier Press had been invited to a luncheon at Edna's Sunfish Lake cottage. I almost shook with anticipation at meeting my idol; yet, I was worried too. What if, in person, Edna was far less than I had imagined her to be? What if she fell off the pedestal I had put her on for so many years?

The magic unfolded as we drove along the winding gravel roads, through the secluded woods to Sunfish Lake. And, as I knew it would be, Edna's cottage was perfect—cluttered with books, paintings, cards and flowers from well-wishers. And Edna herself? I needn't have feared disappointment. She was so warm and chatty and had that rare knack of immediately putting strangers at their ease. I'll admit that in my imagination, I pictured the two of us—Edna reading a good book; me with my knitting, passing the day in quiet friendship

Driving back to the city, I was quietly content, still reveling in the perfection of Sunfish Lake. A faded picture of that day reminds me that it wasn't a dream.

Hilde Slezak
Waterloo
December 2006

---

1. Ruby Cress, *Haven't Any News. Ruby's Letters from the 50's*. ed. Edna Staebler (Waterloo: Wilfrid Laurier Press, 1995.)

Jean Wright

Jean Wright of Morningside Village in New Hamburg has worn many hats in her lifetime—singer, dancer, award-winning actress and sailboat racer. In 1978, we see her at the Waterloo Farmers' Market in another role— as a vendor of her knitting. It's from this vantage point that Jean encounters Edna Staebler. Like most who met Edna, Jean's memory of this meeting has lingered over the years.

As usual, at 6 a.m. on a Saturday morning, the market is a hive of activity as vendors prepare for the expected crowd of visitors. The aroma of fresh baking fills the air; the vivid colours of farm fresh fruits and vegetables paint a colourful portrait of Waterloo County at its best. The food vendors attract the big crowds, but craft vendors such as myself are never lonely either.

After I've arranged my display of scarves, mittens, toques, sweaters and infant wear on the counter of my stall, I sit back, knitting needles clacking, waiting for customers to drop by. I enjoy watching the crowd, and after 5 years as a market vendor, I'm often rewarded by seeing old familiars amongst the wash of strangers.

On this morning I spot a face in the crowd that calls to my attention. I can't put the face to a name, but I have the notion that this small, middle-aged, bespectacled woman should be familiar to me. She seems to be drawing a crowd herself, as dozens of Saturday morning shoppers stop to say hello, or shake her hand.

She's approaching my stall. Who is she? I take the opportunity to look closer and make a study of her face. It's a pleasant one—neither beautiful nor unattractive, and somewhat asymmetrical. No doubt past middle age, the woman's skin is still youthfully delicate, with fine lines, like crumpled velvet, patterning her complexion. But it's her eyes— sparkling and bright, that set her apart from others in the crowd. These eyes convey an interest and attentiveness to all that goes around her.

Curiously, her face calls to mind an "apple head" doll, and in the privacy of my imagination this is what I call her.

Surprisingly, she stops in front of me and smiles. Immediately, I'm drawn to her, this apple head doll lady, and I want to be her friend. She carefully inspects my wares, then asks me about yarn and style. "A knitter too," I appraise, and note that her voice is soft, yet strong. I'm disappointed when she moves on.

A Special Gift

The next Saturday market, my husband John accompanies me. We sit chatting and waiting. I'm surprised to see the lady again, and I whisper to John: "Here she comes; my apple head doll lady." His brow furrows at this curious name and he leans closer. "That's Edna Staebler, Jean. Don't you know?" The veil of recognition lifts. Of course! Edna Staebler! I had read articles in the paper about this famous writer who lives right on our doorstep.

My heart quickens when she approaches us again. No longer just my apple head doll lady, she's a celebrity in my midst. I hope that my manner doesn't belie my anticipation of talking to her. I needn't have worried. Edna's down to earth, "real folks" manner immediately put me at my ease. We exchange small pleasantries, woman to woman, knitter to knitter.

"I'll take this baby outfit," she offers, choosing a white bonnet, sweater and booties. "I'm off to visit Pierre Berton, and this is a gift for his first grandchild." She's quite happy with her purchase and says good bye. In the blink of an eye, she disappears again into the crowd. It's been a singular morning. I delight in the knowledge that Pierre Berton's first grandchild will greet the world, snug and warm in my handiwork.

I closed my market booth sometime after this and moved on to new ventures. My path never crossed Edna's again. But from time to time, I would think of her, my little apple head doll lady, and was glad I had known her—even for a short space in time.

Jean Wright
New Hamburg
November 2006

Marylu McGrath and Marilyn Berge

Growing up in "Mennonite Country," southwest of Kitchener-Waterloo, Marilyn Berge knew all about Edna Staebler. Her interest in Edna continued after she moved to Vancouver in 1976. A friend knowing this presented Marilyn with Food that Really Schmecks *for her birthday. From then on, every birthday was an occasion for another of Edna's popular cookbooks to join Marilyn's collection.*

In 1990, Marilyn returned to Ontario—Kitchener-Waterloo to be exact, and her love of "all things Edna" continued. By now, her partner Marylu McGrath was also an enthusiastic member of the Edna Staebler fan club!

Both Marilyn and I had seen, and admired Peter Etril Snyder's painting of Edna, titled "Edna at Home," which hung in the Kitchener Public Library. I had, especially, fallen in love with it. It was delightful the way the artist had incorporated pieces of Edna's world into the painting, like her cats, her books and her knitted mice.

Without me knowing it, Marilyn decided that a print of the painting would be a wonderful present for me on my 50th birthday. This would occur in 2002. She went to Peter Etril Snyder's Gallery and Studio in Waterloo to make inquiries about purchasing a reproduction.

Peter was there that day, and Marilyn talked to him. Apparently reproductions of the painting hadn't been created yet, but her interest in purchasing one was enough to get Peter busy making the prints. So, my copy was numbered 2/500. Apparently the studio always keeps the first copy.

Only One Thing Better

The birthday portrait was a happy addition to our collection of Edna books at home. The only thing better would have been to talk to Edna in person. With this fond wish in mind, Marilyn wrote to Edna asking if we could come and visit her. One day, the phone rang and the caller said that she was Edna Staebler. She'd be delighted to meet us.

And so, a few days later, two very excited fans set out for Sunfish Lake. Edna welcomed us into her home like old friends. I remember feeling star-struck in her presence at first, but she was so down to earth and natural, I soon relaxed and enjoyed our conversation.

When the talk turned to the Etril Snyder portrait, Edna told us how apprehensive she had been, at the time, about how the painting portrayed her. She hadn't seen it, at all, while Peter was working on it, and she had become worried how she should respond when the work was unveiled for the first time. What if she didn't like it?

Apparently, she consulted her friend Gerry Noonan about her worries. Gerry related to her an anecdote involving Picasso and a portrait he had painted for the writer Gertrude Stein. Stein didn't like the painting and had said to Picasso: "It doesn't look like me." Picasso replied: "Oh, but it *will*, madam, it *will*." The 3 of us roared with laughter.

Refreshments with Edna

After more chit-chat, Edna asked us if we'd like to stay for tea and cake. Would we? Tea? Cake? From the *Schmeck's* lady? How much more wonderful could this afternoon be? What Marilyn and I didn't know, being "Edna novices," was that Edna didn't bake much anymore. It seems that visitors usually brought goodies with them and these donations were what Edna fed to her hordes of visitors. But despite Edna's busy social calendar, the supply was still more than the demand, and Edna stored much of the food in her basement freezer. Some remained there for a good while.

For our visit, she had pulled out a lemon cake. I had gone into the kitchen to help her and couldn't help but notice that, according to its package, the cake was well past its "best before" date. I had to stifle a chuckle. Edna Staebler, world-famous cookbook author hauling stale cake out of her freezer!

But this didn't seem to faze Edna in the slightest and my own concerns quickly vanished. Edna was well into her 90's, and was the picture of health, so I figured that Marilyn and I had little to fear from the cake. Edna whipped it into the microwave—wondering aloud how long she should leave it in. It turned out to be delicious, and we all lived to greet another day!

We still think of ourselves as Edna's biggest fans, and are grateful that we got the opportunity to know—even a bit, this remarkable woman.

Marylu McGrath
Kitchener
April, 2007

Shirley Schweitzer

For many years, Shirley Schweitzer and her late husband Paul ran Schweitzer Haus Bed and Breakfast in Hawkesville, west of St. Jacobs. The Schweitzers were also avid bridge players and often found themselves partnered with Norm and Ralph Hodgson, Edna Staebler's sister and brother-in-law. It was courtesy of this connection that they became acquainted with Edna.

Like so many of Edna's visitors to Sunfish Lake, Paul and Shirley also came bearing gifts of food. But Paul's gift would hold certain significance for their hostess.

Paul loved to bake yeast breads and buns. His favourite was the "Neil's Harbour White Bread" recipe from Edna's *Food that Really Schmecks* cookbook. Although he had tried many other yeast bread recipes in other books, even all the other breads in the various *Schmecks* series, none, in his opinion, matched "Neil's Harbour White Bread." He baked it regularly to serve to our B and B guests. Oh! They loved it—especially for breakfast as toast, with homemade jams and jellies. It makes my mouth water just remembering it!

So, on our first visit to Sunfish, Paul decided he would bring a loaf of the "Neil's Harbour" for Edna to enjoy. He was a little nervous giving it to her, Edna being the famous cook and all. But she loved it and gave him warm compliments. It seemed to really please her that it was *his* favourite, as it was hers—although she admitted that she didn't bake bread anymore.

The Circle Connects

One Saturday sometime later, we invited Edna, Norm and Ralph to visit our home. Our other visitor was Matthias Martin. Now Matthias was an interesting gent—an Old Order Mennonite. He worked with leather and was a skilled harness maker. We didn't have horses, or harnesses, but we did have an old trunk which had needed new leather straps. Matthias was the one who made them. So we got to know him and enjoyed his company. He made an interesting "six-some" to our party.

It's funny how the things connected around Edna. Matthias' daughter was Nancy Martin, who was a great friend of Edna's. Nancy was no less interesting than her father. And so, the circle around Edna seemed to go around and around.

But back to the Saturday Brunch! With our party of 6, Paul offered another of his specialties, Chelsea Buns. These too were taken from the *Schmecks* section on yeast breads. And along with this treat, Paul served various cheeses, home made jams and jellies. Edna took one bite of the Chelsea Bun and declared, "These are the best Chelsea Buns I've ever eaten."

Paul was delighted to hear this, and asked her: "Can I tell our Bed and Breakfast guests you endorse them?" Edna said we could. And we did! Many, many times. It always surprised us how many of our out-of-town guests knew of Edna and her cookbooks. I think people had read *Schmecks* from coast to coast.

Edna never knew how much her compliments had meant to Paul. She just had a knack of making people feel good about themselves. Both Paul and I were blessed to have known her, and we cherished every moment that we had in her company.

Shirley Schweitzer
Waterloo
April 2007

Catharine Vassiliadis

October 3, 2002 saw writer Cathy Vassiliadis tuning into the popular CBC Radio program "As It Happens." Of particular interest to her was a telephone interview conducted by host Mary Lou Findlay with Edna Staebler. The chat was a timely one, as Edna had made front page news the day before, by turning down a request to appear on the late night "Jay Leno Show."

Some time before the interview, Cathy and her husband Minas, who was an old friend of Edna had scheduled a visit to Sunfish Lake. The couple eagerly anticipated getting more detailed information from Edna about the "snub." Cathy recalls the occasion:

It appears that Jay Leno's interest had sprung from a story[1] that had run in the Kitchener *Record* about Edna's life accomplishments and the passion with which she still looked forward to each and every day. Accompanying the story was a stunning photograph of Edna taken on her dock. Edna was dressed in a royal blue sweater and Sunfish Lake was behind her.

The article had been picked up by an internet wire service and caught by the Leno team in Hollywood, who had issued the invitation to Edna by phone. The show would fly her to California and pay all expenses for her appearance.

Edna's reception to the caller must have been a startling one. Not only had she never seen the "Jay Leno Show," but she'd never heard of Jay Leno! While Edna informed the caller that it was doubtful if she would come, she did promise to watch the show that night. If the caller wished to telephone her tomorrow, a firm decision could be made.

Tuning in to Leno

Edna's first impressions were pretty negative. "All these people in the audience were so noisy, cheering and catcalls and yelling." Edna was disgusted with the performance. She remarked to her cat, Mally, who had also stayed up to watch the spectacle, that they were both "quiet people" who wouldn't like the hubbub that surrounded Mr. Leno and his guests. When Leno's representative called back the next day, Edna's answer was a firm "thanks, but no thanks."

In the aftermath of her refusal of Jay Leno, Edna pondered greater issues. She wondered to friends why there seemed to be more fuss made when she turned down Jay Leno than when she was awarded the Order of Canada? And why she received at least 35 phone calls from family and friends when the story broke. Was this American with the big chin, (Edna compared him, unfavourably, to Brian Mulroney), really such a big deal?

Looking Forward to Edna, in Person
There is power in the radio, to be sure, but there is much more to learn from the physical presence, the body language and the personal attributes of the story-teller. So, I looked forward to seeing the look on Edna's face, how her eyes blazed or how she held her hands as she related the Leno story—as I was sure she would—over tea and muffins, in her living room.

And Edna did not disappoint me. "Why would I want to travel for 5 hours on an airplane for that kind of experience when I have everything I want here?" she questioned.

As Edna spoke, I looked past her shoulder, as she sat in her favourite chair by the window. There was the patio, with its half-dozen bird feeders, and the constant entertainment provided by Mr. Upside Down Nuthatch, Mr. Downy Woodpecker, and the Chickadee families. Here's Mr. Squirrel, being thwarted in his attempt to get nuts from the squirrel-proof feeder; and Mr. Chipmunk who isn't!

Nothing Needed, Past Edna's World
Beyond the patio, the grass expanse, flanked by large trees, sloped to the bleached wood dock and the steel blue lake. Indoors, from my vantage point in Edna's cozy, cluttered living room, the sun porch was visible. It was a summer place, too

cold for the chill of October. Still, it still held the books and magazines that had filled Edna's summer days; the flowers brought by friends; the comfortable chairs for summer living, and the inevitable dish of hard candies.

And then Edna showed me her trusty Milk Calendar, the "personal assistant" that kept track of the armies of people who came to visit her. I was sure that the number of appointments in any October week was greater than any corporate executive had to face in a month—maybe two.

And now I fully understood Edna's rejection of Jay Leno. Why would she head to the land of commercial Hollywood, when her own world was so complete, with its ever-changing lake, the surrounding green space, and the creatures who came to call. Why would she want to miss the telephone calls and in-person visits—even for a few days—of her friends, family and colleagues, for a few fleeting moments of fame on American television? Yes, I understood Edna Staebler perfectly.

What power this elderly lady had. She was surely the epitome of all that is good about a long life, productively spent, in Canada. At a passionate 96 years young, Edna showed the wisdom, the culture, the humanity and the intellect that we all aspire to as Canadians.

And she kept living fully until her last breath. In another 40 years, I hope I am just like her.

Cathy Vassiliadis
Durham
January 2007

---

1. The article, "Too Busy to Slow Down," written by this author appeared in the *Record* on August 31, 2002. Section G, p. 1.

Trustee Catherine Fife

After graduating from Teacher's College (OCE) in 1932, Edna found employment as a teacher at the Ingersoll High School. It was not a match made in heaven, and Edna remained there for only one year. Although her teaching career was short, she remained committed to the welfare of children throughout her life.

From the birthday parties she held for neighbourhood children on Simeon Street, through to the scholarships she sponsored at area universities, Edna's light shone around young people. Wilfrid Laurier President, Dr. Robert Rosehart observed of Edna: "It was no mistake that many of those who became close to Edna were much younger than her. She was at her best when young people were around, and seemed to gain energy from them."

Edna Staebler as an inspiration to youth was recognized in May 2007 when the Waterloo Region District School Board announced that its newest school, which will open in September 2008, will be named Edna Staebler Public School.[1] The school to be built in the Clair Hills area, west of Waterloo, is nearby to Edna's former home on Sunfish Lake.

Board Trustees Catherine Fife, Kathleen Woodcock and Board Chair Andrea Mitchell had spearheaded the naming process. Trustee Fife reveals the rationale behind the selection.

Whenever a new public school is built in our region, the school board solicits suggestions from the public for a name. It's the Board's belief that as schools have gained their strength from the communities that surround them, so too should those communities be involved in their naming.

Fifty-eight people sent in suggestions—and their rationale for the name of the new school. Forty–three of these were in honour of Edna Staebler. So the choice was an easy one for us to make.

Excerpts from two of the nomination letters for Edna Staebler Public School follow:

"Edna was a strong local female role model. She broke many archetypes/stereotypes of her generation; she was a renowned Canadian author; she established an award to encourage other Canadian authors through Wilfrid Laurier University, and was awarded the Order of Canada. More importantly, Edna was a wonderful woman who had a zest for life, and she was born, raised and died in Waterloo Region."

"Edna was a pillar in our community. Her quiet manner and extraordinary thirst for knowledge and new experiences make her a perfect role model for young people (especially young girls). She was an accomplished woman—ahead of her time."

The Community Speaks

We were so pleased that Edna's place in the community which she loved was recognized. Schools should send a message to their communities about strength and courage and commitment to what they believe in. Edna did that through her writing, and through the way she led her life.

And that life had not always been easy for her. She had often needed to rise above disappointments and heartaches. But she did that through strength of character and determination. And so Edna became a role model by living simply, kindly and with integrity. What better example to guide youngsters through their early years?

Edna's name will now be carried on into the future. It's my hope that every Edna Staebler Public School student will study who Edna Staebler was, and how she contributed to her community. What better way to teach than through living history?

Catherine Fife
Kitchener
May 2007

Edna:
The Friend

Edna: the Friend

Barbara Naylor
"No doubt with a twinkle in his eye, Gzowski countered: 'But Edna how do you know?'"

Jean Williams
"Edna seemed to be on the go all the time, taking an interest in every aspect of the village."

Eva Bauman
"I recall Janet Berton getting quite excited when she saw the hairpins that my girls and I used to hold our hair into buns."

Trish Stewart and Madelene Dewar
"No showy clothes or jewellery for Edna...she was a Thrift Store kind of girl."

Nancy Martin
"And while the story Edna told was beautiful in itself...in telling it to me, her voice had changed."

Irene Schmidt
"I knew that I just had to meet her and talk to her about Cape Breton."

Teresa Huegel
"Edna never said things in a 'poor me' tone of voice. She was matter-of-fact, and knew that for her, the end was near."

Barbara Naylor

Barbara Naylor traces her meeting with Edna to the mid-1970's. The Naylor family had a house guest who was an aspiring writer. A call to Waterloo County's most celebrated author, Edna Staebler, resulted in an invitation to the would-be writer and her hostess to Sunfish Lake. "The rest, as they say is history," Barbara laughs.

Over the next 35 years, Barbara would regularly make the trip to Sunfish Lake, sometimes alone, sometimes with her young daughter, Pam. She became one of Edna's most trusted friends.

A woman with a penchant for off-the-beaten-path travel, including trekking the Chilkoot Pass in Canada's far north; to the former Mustang Kingdom, now part of Nepal, and China's Karakoram Range on the border with Pakistan, Barbara would always make Sunfish an early stop on her list of "tell me about your trip" visits.

Barbara's most recent adventure to Ethiopia, Jordan and Egypt took place shortly after Edna's death in September 2006. She recalls the strangeness she felt on her return. "I had to stop myself a hundred times from saying: 'I'll have to tell that to Edna.'"

She pulls from her bag of tales, 3 stories about her friend.

Armed with a Rolling Pin

After an evening out, Edna arrived home to find an upset. As she approached her house, a glitter on the sidewalk caught her eye. It was one of her necklaces. Several other pieces of jewellery were strewn about, too. It was obvious that her home had been burglarized.

Edna entered her house cautiously. She was relieved to find that no one was there and that it hadn't been ransacked. But a window had been broken as the thief let himself in. A quick survey of the home's contents revealed that only a few items were missing—liquor and jewellery.

Immediately Edna put in a call to the Waterloo police station and they sent an investigating officer out to Sunfish. He surmised that, given that Edna's home had been the only targeted robbery in the neighbourhood, the thief had known of her absence that night.

It appeared too that the crook knew his jewellery. After stuffing all Edna's glitter, willy-nilly into a bag before leaving, he had decided to separate the costume from more valuable pieces. The former articles were left behind on the sidewalk. Beyond that, the policeman had little to offer and advised Edna that recovery of the goods was unlikely. His most prominent concern was Edna's safety and security.

Given that Edna was in her mid-80's and lived alone, the officer encouraged her to sleep elsewhere. He would be glad to drive her to a friend's home. Now it was pretty obvious that the policeman didn't know Edna. Grandmotherly she might appear to some; underneath the docile exterior beat the heart of a lion. No way was she going to sleep somewhere else that night, she informed him. It was *her* home, and she'd be darned if she was going to leave it. Besides, what would her cat think? No, she would remain on guard. However, she could use a hand boarding up the broken window.

So Edna prepared herself for bed, said goodnight to the cat and tucked herself in. She kept a rolling pin under the covers, just in case. Woe be to the burglar who came face to face with Edna Staebler!

Her only concession to improved security was to later place a sticker on her door warning other would-be thieves that her home was protected by a security system. Only Edna's friends knew that it was a clever ruse.

Edna and Peter
Edna was a favourite of broadcaster Peter Gzowski and he interviewed her on several occasions on his Morningside radio show. One of her last interviews with him was when she was in her mid-90's. Edna had insisted on driving to Toronto herself for the chat.

The conversation and banter between the two consummate pros was delightful and wide ranging. Gzowski congratulated Edna on her recent induction into the rank of the Order of Canada (an honour Gzowski held himself). He also questioned her on the selection of the latest winner of the Edna Staebler Award for Creative Nonfiction.

Then playfully, Gzowski posed the inevitable question: "So Edna, are there books within you yet to be written, at your ripe young age?" Ready for the probe, Edna volleyed, "Peter, I'm not immortal, you know." No doubt, with a twinkle in his eye, Gzowski countered, "But Edna, how do you know?"

With this, the familiar Morningside theme signaled the end of the show. There was no sign-off, just the last sweet exchange when time stood still and listeners (and friends) grasped the significance of Peter's query.

Where Time Stood Still
As a little girl, my daughter Pam always wanted to come with me for a visit to Sunfish Lake. "Can I come too, Mommy?" when I'd announce that I was going to that bucolic cottage by the lake. Promising the others that we'd be back in less than 2 hours, we always stayed 3 or 4. It was just so hard to leave that world.

Even before Edna's house came into view, our moods had shifted from city hurry to Sunfish Lake serenity. The feeling had came on gradually, as the car left the paved highways, approached the "hole in the trees" and leisurely continued on along the country lane. By the time Edna's home came into sight, not an ounce of work-a-day stress lingered.

Over the afternoon our conversation would range widely. Always stimulating, it covered news of the day, travels—hers and mine; Edna's recent writing projects, and others' new book releases. The latter were out on display, in easy reach. Refreshments were always offered and gladly received. Tea for Edna and I, something cold for Pam, and a sweet for all of us.

And as we sipped, and talked, a steady parade of Edna's beloved woodland creatures—birds, squirrels, chipmunks and the occasional raccoon passed by her lakeside window. Edna's cats, depending on their mood that day, would also offer comment on the procession, or remain on Edna's lap, content and purring. "Tomorrow will bring the show again, so no need to waste a good cat nap," was their attitude.

Pam listened quietly to our conversation; she looked at Edna's latest books, enjoyed the cats, the birds at the feeder and the changing water patterns on the lake. As Edna's world opened before her, Pam saw, listened and absorbed sights, sounds, and thoughts. Those visits left a lasting impression on my young daughter—perhaps more than she or I, even Edna knew, at the time. Not long ago, Edna remarked to me that she thought her "sweetly mysterious."

For many years after she was grown and left home, Pam continued to visit Edna. As soon as she stepped in the cottage, memories of our visits, long-ago, came flooding back. For little had changed—the furniture, the pictures on the walls, or the friendly clutter. Entering Edna's world, one could believe that time had stood still.

Now living thousands of miles away from her childhood home, my grown-up daughter grieved the news of Edna's passing. Like me, she mourned the loss of this gentle, wise and quietly determined woman who valued friendship and loyalty; one who lived a simple life, in harmony with nature.

Barbara Naylor
Waterloo
March 2007

Jean Williams (nee Ingraham) and Fred Williams

Edna first visited Neil's Harbour,[1] a picturesque fishing village on the north shore of Cape Breton Island, in 1945. She returned again for 6 weeks in 1947. Her hosts for the second stay were Clara May and Henry Ingraham, and their family of 12 children. Over the years, Edna would become close to the Ingrahams. She returned several times to visit, cementing her bond to the family and to Neil's Harbour.

Clara May passed away in 1976, but Edna remained in contact with several of her children and grandchildren. One daughter, Jean (Williams) now 82, continues to live in Neil's Harbour. With her son Fred 61, of Ingonish, Cape Breton Island, a retired secondary school teacher, Jean offers recollections of Edna Staebler.

I believe I first met Edna in the summer of 1945. My husband, Henry and I were living with Hubert and Alice Williams, my in-laws. It was a lovely day to do the wash— a nice breeze, and good for drying. I took the baby, Fred, and went out to the clothesline. As I was hanging the clothes, I noticed a strange woman sitting on the veranda over at Christie Pearl's, our next-door neighbours.

I got to the end of the line near the fence and the woman came over to say 'hello.' She was such a happy-looking person, and seemed so interested in talking about the village. That was the beginning of a very long friendship[2] between me and Edna Staebler.

I saw Edna many times during her stay in Neil's Harbour that year. She liked to walk up and down the gravel roads of the village. It was pleasant to do this then, as there weren't many vehicles. Edna seemed to be on the go all the time, taking an interest in every aspect of village life. It wasn't long before she made many friends—me included.

One day, I took her up to see Mother and Father (Clara May and Henry Ingraham) and they too became lifelong friends.

After this, when Edna returned for visits, she always stayed with them. She became part of the family.

Edna had so many interests. She wanted to know how life was changing in the village, with many young people going off to Ontario. This gave her the idea for a story which she wrote about my sister Maggie,[3] who was leaving for Toronto, to find work.

She was also interested in Mother's cooking, and she used Clara May's bread recipe in one of her cookbooks.[4]

The Sword Fishing Excursion

Edna was particularly interested in the fishing industry and spent many hours "over at the shore" (a local expression meaning the wharves and fish houses). She had a difficult time, at first, with the dialect. Most people in both Neil's Harbour and New Haven originally came from Newfoundland. They have a strong dialect and used expressions not heard in other parts of Cape Breton. It took Edna much of that first visit to understand some of the references, but soon she could follow the conversations very well.

Edna's interest in the shore and fishing got her once into a bit of stew because she wrote about it in one of her stories. You see, women weren't supposed to be around the boats and wharves. There's a belief that it's bad luck for a woman to go out in a fishing boat— just as it's bad luck to turn a hatch cover over on the deck. Of course Edna, being curious, and wanting to write about people and their livelihood, wanted desperately to go out in a boat.

Now, I'm not sure how she managed to talk one of the sword fishermen, Freeman Seymour and his crew into taking her for a day's fishing, but she did. There was the "bad luck" factor and also the bathroom situation. A woman on a man's boat has a problem! Anyway, Edna persevered and had a wonderful day on the water. I don't think they got a swordfish, but she had the experience. She went on the water a few more times during future visits.

A Story for a Magazine

Edna didn't visit us every year, but she always wrote. In the early 60's, she came in late November or December and spent over a month in the village.[5] She wanted to do a story on my family for *Chatelaine Magazine*.

I was a little shy doing it at first, because I didn't know what was involved. But I put my faith in Edna and said it was OK. She spent a lot of time at our house asking questions about our daily routines and how we managed our lives. Money was so scarce and I don't think Edna ever realized before how difficult it was for us to make ends meet. She asked us lots of questions, but she never got in the way. Besides, Edna was such a good friend, and was so nice to talk to.

Other times, she took pictures, did her writing, and took her walks around, just like she did during her summer visits.

A Connection with Fred

My son, Fred was a little nervous while Edna was doing the *Chatelaine* story because she spent some time at his school taking pictures. She also photographed him playing road hockey and doing other activities. I guess, being a young teenager, he didn't want the attention. But Edna was so good with children; it was hard for them, Fred included, *not* to like her.

She took an interest the youngsters' school work and their hobbies too. Fred liked drawing and Edna sent him a "Jon Nagy" art set one Christmas. It was the best thing anyone could have given him. He spent hours with it, and it stirred in him an interest in drawing and painting which he has to this very day.

Their connection continued when Fred became the teacher-librarian at Cabot High School in Neil's Harbour. During one of her visits in the 1970's, Fred took Edna to the school and showed her the library. From that day on, she made it a point to support it.

Every year, she shipped books from the Kitchener-Waterloo University Women's Club book sale to him. In later years, she donated her advance from the republishing of *Cape Breton Harbour* to the library. It was a wonderful help to the school, because their book budget was so little.

Keeping the Connection

In later years, Edna's visits to Neil's Harbour became fewer. There were things going on in her life that kept her busy in Ontario and other parts of the world. But she always wrote to tell us what was happening and where she was traveling.

In the late 1980's, I took a trip to Ontario to visit several of my brothers and sisters who live there. We went up to Sunfish Lake to see Edna. I was so glad to do this because she always had talked about the lake so much. It was a lovely visit, and Edna and I had a wonderful day going back over 40 years in our memories.

I think that was the last time I saw her. Still, we talked on the phone several times a year. She always kept her interest in the village, and wanted an update on the people she knew. Of course, Edna lived longer than most people, and many of them had passed on.

Before she died, Edna made a bequest to the Cabot High School Library for the amount of $25,000. This would be used to buy books for the students. What a good friend she was to Neil's Harbour and to all of us. It's why people here keep alive the memories of our dear friend Edna Staebler.

Jean Williams and Fred Williams
Neil's Harbour, Cape Breton Island
June 2007

---

1. The story of Edna's connection to Neil's Harbour is told in Edna's book, *Cape Breton Harbour* (Toronto: McClelland &Stewart, 1972).

2. Edna, born in 1906, was 19 years older than Jean.

3. Edna Staebler, *Whatever Happened to Maggie and Other People I've Known* (Toronto: McClelland and Stewart, 1983; reprinted by McGraw-Hill Ryerson as Maggie in 1990)

4. Edna Staebler, "Neil's Harbour White Bread" in *Food that Really Schmecks* Toronto: McClelland and Stewart, 1968.

5. Edna's visit coincided with Keith Staebler receiving treatment for alcoholism. His physicians had advised Edna to leave the house for an extended period of time so Keith could not return. This period of time discussed at length in Veronica Ross's biography of Edna. *To Experience Wonder: Edna Staebler: A Life* (Toronto: Dundurn Press, 2003), p.p. 182-183.

Eva Bauman

Eva Bauman first met Edna on her parents' farm, in the mid-1960's. At the time, she was a young woman of 18, and Edna was a fan of fresh farm produce. Edna often stopped there for her purchases. Always chatty and friendly, she would usually linger awhile, sharing a cup of tea with the ladies of the house, including Eva and her sister Hannah. The friendship continued after both sisters married and set up their own households. In the coming years, they would come to know Edna as their "dear and special friend."

Eva's most vivid recollections of her friend concern food. The first is a luncheon held in Edna's honour; the second, near the end of Edna's life is a tea party at Columbia Forest Long Term Care.

A Party for Edna

Edna turned 85 in 1991, and I wanted to have a party for her.[1] But her birthday was in January—not a good time for a get-together, especially in the country. So I postponed it till the end of September when the heat of the summer was over. I asked Edna to invite a couple of her other friends to come along. She decided to ask Janet Berton, Pierre's wife, and the writer June Callwood. She thought that they'd enjoy the opportunity to have real Waterloo County Mennonite cooking.

Now in our homes, the main meal is eaten at lunchtime. And so it would be for Edna's party. And what does a Mennonite cook serve a friend who is a famous cookbook writer? Well of course, what we'd serve any special guest! Although I can't remember every detail of what we ate that day, I can guess, knowing what are my specialties. For the meat, surely our home-made pork sausage, with new potatoes, cooked and sliced, then served with cream; fresh corn and garden peas. Probably coleslaw, and a jellied salad too. And of course, home-made bread or dinner rolls.

In our culture, preserves always follow the main course and go before the dessert. These are usually strawberries or pears, picked on our farm and done up in my kitchen. No tinned fruit in a Mennonite farm woman's pantry!

The guests would need to save some room for dessert too. My specialty is caramelized pudding, with whipped dairy cream; and also "jam-jam" cookies. They're put together like a sandwich with apple butter in-between. Whether there was pie or not, I'm not sure, but if there was, it would have been cherry or raspberry.

Remembering Janet and June

My memories of June Callwood and Janet Berton have lasted longer than the details of the meal. June was very interested in the quilts that were sitting around. She wanted to know if we had made them and how long they took. So I led her upstairs to see the others. How many were there? I can't recall, but probably more than a dozen. I can still see the look on her face when she saw all of them.

I explained to her that learning to quilt and sew is an important part of a Mennonite girl's education. It's expected that by the time each girl is married, she'd have stitched (with help from other women) at least 8 quilts. As I have 4 daughters, all unmarried at the time, that's why my house looked like a quilt store!

It's funny the things that stick in your mind. I recall Janet Berton getting quite excited when she saw the hairpins that my girls and I used to hold our hair into buns.

"Where on earth did you get those pins?" she asked. "I've looked all over Toronto for them!"

"We get them at John Martin's Country Store," was my answer.

"Where is that? Is it close?"

I thought she was going to get right up and go!

"It's on the Linwood Road," and I suggested that if she drove me, I'd take her there.

So Janet Berton and I drove up country to buy some hair pins. I think that little trip was almost better for her than the meal she had eaten.

They are good memories of a very special day. And now June Callwood is gone. I'm happy that I had the chance to meet her and welcome her into our home.

Bibs!

After Edna moved to Columbia Forest, several of us made a point of having a tea party for her, every so often. We'd bring everything, including the tea pot, nice tea cups, napkins, plates, and, of course, a special sweet treat for the occasion. A favourite was "Peanut Butter Pie." Oh, Edna loved it!

She was always happy to have her afternoon tea in a "grown up" manner too. "They (Columbia Forest staff) make us wear bibs at meals," she'd grumble. But this was one of the few things that Edna *would* ever complain about. Being grouchy just wasn't part of who she was.

But by now, Edna seemed just tired. She just didn't have that "Edna spark" that I had always known. She was, after all, a century old! And where she'd always been the chatty one— full of news about the people she knew, and the places she'd seen, she was now quiet, taking in the conversation going on around her.

"Nothing exciting ever happens here," she'd laugh, "so I won't say much, and just listen." And she did—with both her ears, the way she'd always listened.

Eva Bauman
Heidelberg
April 2007

---

1. Eva's recollection of Edna's luncheon varies on certain points from June Callwood's.

Trish Stewart and Madelene Dewar
for Dr. Gerald Noonan

Gerry Noonan and Edna Staebler took to each other like honey bees to magnolia blossoms. Dr. Gerry, a professor of English Literature at Wilfrid Laurier University (formerly Waterloo Lutheran) taught a popular creative writing class. He liked to bring in published writers as models of inspiration to his students. Edna Staebler, award-winning journalist, and successful author of **Food that Really Schmecks** *was invited, on numerous occasions to the class. The friendship which evolved between them stemmed from these occasions.*

But academic and teacher was only one of Gerry's identities. An extrovert and "bon vivant," Gerry also relished his role of unofficial social convener of the small university, and frequently arranged outings for faculty and staff. Gerry's bus trips to such venues as the Stratford Festival, the Art Gallery of Ontario, or area "watering holes" were legend, and booked up almost as soon as they were offered. "The more the merrier" was Gerry's motto and he'd routinely extend an invitation to Edna to come along.

When Gerry and Edna learned that each shared the same birth date of January 15 (as did Gerry's sister Madelene Dewar), this too became an occasion for an annual celebration.

Trish Stewart, Gerry's step-daughter, and his sister, Madelene reminisce about the bond that grew up between Edna and Gerry.

Gerry was a larger than life person. He loved the limelight, and went out of the way to be flamboyantly noticed. He'd be the guy who stands up in a pub and begins to sing; the guy who wears the blinking bow tie; the character who does magic tricks and wears crazy hats. And people of all sorts, of all interests and professions, were drawn to him for it. Gerry was like the centre of a wheel, and his many friends and associates radiated out from him.

Edna's personality matched Gerry's perfectly. He was intrigued by her, and loved to hear the stories she told about her research for her *Maclean's* articles—the ones that had her living with fishermen, Mennonites, miners and so on. In a crowd of people, he would frequently "promote" Edna, suggesting she tell this story or that. She liked talking too, so they were great with each other.

Platonic Dates

There was no physical relationship between Edna and Gerry. First, she was much older than him.[1] Secondly, he was a married man. But there was absolutely no jealousy on Pam's (Noonan) part about Edna. In fact, she liked her very much and would often come out to Sunfish to visit.

This convenient situation allowed Gerry to be the arm for Edna to hang on to when she needed a "date" at a social function—a date with no strings attached.

Yet Edna's diary entry for February 7, 2000, reveals that at one time she might have contemplated taking her friendship with her much younger best friend to another stage. In one of her diary entries, Edna confides:

> "Ours was a strange relationship, in a way, a true friendship, not an emotional attachment tho' truly loving. If I hadn't been 26 years older than Gerry there might have been complications. Gerry—I can't think of my world without him."[2]

A Thrift Store Kind of Girl

As if their similar outgoing personalities, common interests and sense of fun weren't enough to bond them, Gerry and Edna also had similar values. This became evident one time when Pam bought Gerry an expensive watch. She thought he'd love it—being the "flashy guy" he was. But he didn't at all. It was too expensive and he would have preferred to find one he liked at a flea market for $5.

Pam couldn't understand this and was hurt. But Edna did; in fact, she was quite like this herself. No showy clothes or jewellery for Edna, even though she could have afforded anything she wanted. Edna was a "Thrift Store" type of girl.

Still, Gerry had his "dark side." He could be bossy and judgmental, and was quick to tell people how they should be doing things, quicker or better. Most family and some friends had felt his barbs on more than one occasion. But Edna was up on a pedestal for him, and he never tried to tell her how she should be living her life. In fact, I think sometimes she quite intimidated him.

Gerry was diagnosed with liver cancer shortly after he retired in 1995. He was devastated, but once he got his head around it, he decided to fight back. Keeping on a strict regimen of exercise, vitamins and healthy eating, he remained quite active until early 2000. Edna helped his head during this time. Her upbeat personality kept him positive and active.

Then he got very sick and his appearance changed. His skin was a yellowy colour and his weight dropped. For a vain man, this was the hardest blow of all. He refused to go out and refused friends who wanted to come to call. He wouldn't even let Edna see him like this. He'd take her phone calls, but that was all.

Edna suffered greatly from this. She felt so helpless and looked for a way she could do something for him.

In a February 7, 2000 entry in her diary, Edna talks of an idea she is forming to recognize her dear friend:

> "Maybe I could establish a fellowship or scholarship in his name at WLU. I think he'd like that. He should be honoured in some way. He touched so many lives and everyone likes him. He always thought about people and what he could do for them, and even when he was

very busy, he'd give them time and thought and help people he didn't know well—not friends, just people he'd met or taught." [3]

Edna met with us to gauge our reaction to her plan. We thought it was wonderful and gave her the "green light" to go ahead. A short time later, a registered letter from the university, arrived at the house. It was announcing the Gerry Noonan Memorial Scholarship. The award would have a cash value of up to $3000 and would be given each year to a promising student of English Literature or Film Studies at WLU. Of course, Gerry knew that Edna was behind it.

He was totally overwhelmed and very touched by the news, and said that it was the most important gift anyone had ever given him. He called Edna and they talked on the phone for some time. It must have been a very difficult conversation for both of them.

After Gerry died[4] we continued to see Edna from time to time. Each January 15, we remembered her (and Gerry) on our shared birthdays. But we didn't get together, as we had when Gerry was alive. It just didn't seem the same.

Trish Stewart and Madelene Dewar
Bloomingdale,
March 2007

---

1. When Edna and Gerry Noonan met, she was in her late 60's; he was in his mid-40's.

2. Edna Staebler. *Must Write: Edna Staebler's Diaries*, ed. Christl Verduyn (Waterloo: Wilfrid Laurier Press, 2005), p.275.

3. Ibid, p. 276

4. Gerry Noonan passed away on March 15, 2000. He was 68 years of age. Edna made no diary reference to his passing. The reader sees this omission as a mark of Edna's pain in losing her best friend.

Nancy Martin

*Nancy Martin of Hawkesville met Edna through her friend, Eva
Bauman. Over the coming 4 decades, the 3 women would visit often,
drawn together by their common love of good books, good food and
good friendship.*

*She recalls accompanying Eva to Sunfish Lake to meet Edna for
the first time. Of all the vivid memories of that day, it was Edna's
reflections on the mood of the lake that stood out most clearly.*

It was apparent to me from my first visit to Sunfish Lake that
Edna was in tune with nature. She pointed out that the lake
changed its "face" from day to day, depending on the height of
the sun, the winds and, of course, the season.

With considerable delight and wonder, she also told us
about the wildlife that lived all around her—the various birds,
the squirrels, the rabbits and the chipmunks. Edna could
identify all of them and talked of the animals almost as beloved
neighbours. She felt an obligation to look after them too when
winter came, and she made sure there was always food put
out for them. The squirrels were a pesky problem though, and
they'd routinely find ways to climb up the bird feeder and steal
the food.

The inside of Edna's cottage held treasures of a different
sort—paintings, books, curios, china. She took great delight in
showing them to her callers. One of her favourites was a painting
called "Undefeated Tree" that had been done by Linda Johns,
a writer and artist from Nova Scotia. Linda had won the Edna
Staebler Award for Creative Nonfiction for her book *Sharing A
Robin's Life*.

Edna's "Brand" of Friendship

Over the years, my friendship with Edna grew, and I came to
view her as a good friend. I believe that she felt the same about
me. You always felt secure being one of Edna's friends because

you knew that she would never be nice to you to your face, and then talk about you behind your back. But Edna had certain standards for what a friend should be, and she'd let you know them in indirect ways. But I can honestly say that not once in the over 40 years that I knew her, did I ever hear her say a catty or cruel remark about someone, or run down another person. This made me feel that I could trust her totally. I always felt so grateful to her for this.

Edna in Love

How can you pick a favourite memory out of so many over the space of 40 years? I have so many they could fill a book. But if I had to choose, it would be of a call I paid to her at Beechwood Manor in late 2005. She was almost 100. I was aware how Edna had always cherished the calendars that her Swiss friend Alphonse sent her for Christmas each year. On the day of my visit, Edna reminisced about a special time they had had, many years ago, in France.

The day had been a glorious one. She and Alphonse had driven to the mountains for a picnic. They sat right on the wildflowers and had a wondrous view of the valley below, and the Alps in the distance. Alphonse had brought the picnic—bread, cheese and jam in a tube. Edna had never seen "squeezable" jam like this before.

And while the story Edna told was beautiful in itself, I couldn't help but notice how, in telling it to me, her voice had changed. It was young, vibrant and lilting, quite different than it had been before. And as I listened to her talk, I realized that one would never have thought that it was the voice was of a woman born almost a century before. Clearly Edna was enraptured as she relived this very special time in her past when she had been in love. I found it a beautiful moment, more so because she was talking to me, a conservative, unmarried Mennonite woman.

Someone had once told me that Edna was afraid that

Eva and I might have thought badly of her because she had taken a lover. Of course we didn't, but it was so like Edna—caring, considerate and kind, and always respectful of our Mennonite culture.

Lived Too Long
In the last days of her life, Edna talked less and listened more. She was always so glad to see her visitors, but I think we tired her too. One day, she told me that she felt that she had lived too long. I know that she missed the friends who had been part of her life many years ago. Pierre Berton comes to mind. When she talked about Pierre's death, it was one of the few times that I felt she was sad. But then the mood lifted, and she was "Edna" again. The Edna that so many people, including myself loved as a cherished friend.

Nancy Martin
Hawkesville
January 2007

Irene Schmidt

A self-proclaimed woman with "a case of the wanderlust," Irene Schmidt had long wanted to visit Cape Breton Island. She suggested to her husband Wilf that they go east. He preferred to remain at home. Undeterred, Irene decided to strike out on her own and booked a flight to Sydney, Cape Breton Island. On her arrival there, she rented a car and started on her way around the famed Cabot Trail.

Having gone only a short distance on her journey, Irene noticed a highway marker for the settlement of Neil's Harbour, a few miles off the Trail. The name sounded intriguing, so she pointed her car in that direction. Little did she dream that her visit that day would ultimately lead to finding a new friend right in her own backyard.

I stopped to talk to the first person I saw in Neil's Harbour—an old man. Before I could really ask him any questions about the village he said: "D' ye want to see moy knives? I makes them out of swordfish." I was a bit startled, but agreed I would, and he led me into his little house. Thinking back on it, I wonder what made me agree to going in with him. But it never occurred to me to be fearful. Neil's Harbour just didn't seem to be such a place. And so I saw the knives, complimented the man on his workmanship and was on my way.

I absolutely loved Cape Breton—the remote beauty of it, the quaint villages, but most of all the people. Perfect strangers would invite you into their house for a spot of tea—or to see swordfish knives and you'd feel right at home doing so. It was the most wonderful holiday I had ever had. I promised myself I'd be back.

Finding A Jewel

Sometime after I returned home, I was visiting my local library and came across a book called *Cape Breton Harbour*. The author was someone called Edna Staebler. The name meant nothing to me then. No matter; any book about Cape Breton was a real find and I quickly snapped it up. Wasting no time, I dove into the book immediately after I got home. I read.........

> "Now I'm really shaken. I've let myself be abandoned in the bleakest little fishing village on the north coast of Cape Breton Island. I don't even know the name of the place; until an hour ago I didn't know it existed. I can't find in on a map of Nova Scotia. The tourist guidebooks don't mention it; there are no signs on the road pointing the way to it. It simply appeared on a sudden bend of the coast after we had been driving through forest from Ingonish, the spectacular village twelve miles south of this on the Cabot Trail."[1]

The words sent a shiver of excitement through me that I had scarcely felt before. This writer, this Edna Staebler wrote about things that I had seen; she saw the beauty of Cape Breton just as I had. And the place where she stayed was Neil's Harbour. That's where I had talked to the old man with the swordfish knives.

When I read the jacket of the book and realized she lived in Waterloo less than an hour away, I knew that I just *had* to meet her and talk to her about Cape Breton.

"But how to locate her?" I doubt if I'll find her name in the phone book, her being a writer and all. Still, no harm in trying."

"What's this? Edna Staebler, R. R.#3, Waterloo? Her name's here. Should I call? Or will she think me terribly forward?" Heart pounding, I picked up the phone to make my call. A woman with a young-old voice answered.

A Welcome Invitation Made and Accepted

As I had hoped it would be, Edna sounded friendly. After I introduced myself and told her my story, she invited me out to Sunfish Lake for tea a few days later. I counted the hours till then.

Approaching Sunfish, I was as giddy as a school girl on prom night. Edna's welcome was as warm as her voice on the telephone and within no time, we were chatting like old friends. What did we have in common? Neil's Harbour, of course; the man with the swordfish knives; the island and our love for it. It was as if Edna and I had known each other forever.

Before I left, I asked her to sign my copy of *Cape Breton Harbour*. She wrote: "To Irene, my Cape Breton soul mate." It has remained one of my most treasured possessions.

Over the years, I visited Edna often. By the late 1990's, she had curtailed her traveling and was eager to hear about my adventures—especially those about my yearly visits to Cape Breton. But Edna and I had other similar interests too, and when news of the island was told, we turned our conversation to those things.

Both Edna and I were passionate about nature, with a special love for the birds. We'd share news about the visitors to her feeder and mine, and compare strategies about keeping the raiding squirrels away. Edna was all ears about the slide shows that I had begun to present to area school children about the various birds that were our neighbours.

A Friendship that was Meant to Be

I made my last visit to Edna the day she passed away. A year after her death, and I still get quite melancholy about it. But I'm also grateful for the opportunity I had to know her and call her "friend."

It was meant to be that I visited Neil's Harbour on that day, so many years ago. It was meant to be that I picked up *Cape Breton Harbour*; and it was meant to be that I called Edna when better sense told me I shouldn't. And because of these things that were meant to be, I met the most special person that I have ever known.

Irene Schmidt
Cambridge
April 2007

---

1. Edna Staebler, *Cape Breton Harbour* (Toronto: McClelland & Stewart, 1972), p. 9.

Teresa Huegel

Teresa Huegel of Waterloo is the co-owner/manager of Angie's Kitchen and Angie's of St. Agatha restaurants. The latter location, only a short distance from Sunfish Lake, served as the first meeting place between Teresa and Edna. In the 1980's and 1990's, Edna was a regular patron at the popular restaurant, and enjoyed bringing friends there for a down home country meal.

Teresa dates the blossoming of her friendship with Edna to 2003, when Edna moved to Beechwood Manor Retirement Home. She acknowledges that as her relationship with Edna grew, she came to recognize in her friend many of her own late mother Angie Graham's (founder of Angie's Restaurant) characteristics. Teresa calls them both "strong women" who triumphed over adversary.

After Edna stopped driving, I didn't see her at the restaurant for a period of time. Then I heard the news that she had moved to Beechwood Manor because of her failing health. One day, on the spur of the moment driving back home to Waterloo after work, I decided to drop in to say "hi." I wasn't even sure if she'd remember me; that's how little I knew her then!

But, of course, she knew me. It was pretty clear that while the stroke might have affected her physically, she was as sharp as a tack mentally. We had a lovely visit and I promised to drop in again. Over the next year or so, I visited twice a week and we got to know each other well.

A Birthday "Bash"

Edna's 99th birthday was approaching on January 15, 2005, and I decided to have a celebration for her at my home. The guest list would be up to her; I asked her to name the people she wanted to come. The rest she could leave to me.

I'd left all my Christmas decorations up, including the 3 trees I assemble each year—always theme colours of burgundy and gold. I'd hauled out my mom's white linen tablecloths and her elegant Spode dishes for the occasion. The pink colours of the dinnerware blended beautifully with the garlands and decorations. If I must say myself, the atmosphere was magical!

The menu would be chicken and roast beef, and only once as I scurried around preparing for the evening did I get a bit of a panic attack. "Do you *know* who you're cooking for?" I asked myself. "Edna Staebler, Queen of the kitchen!" With some work, I calmed down and reassured myself that Edna was "just folks," like the rest of us.

For the birthday girl, I had bought a silver tiara at the local dollar store and placed horns and sparklers at each place setting. This party was going to be done up right! The guests arrived; then Edna made her appearance, driven by her close friend and neighbour, Kevin Thomason. So now the festivities could begin. It was wonderful to see how happy she was, surrounded by people who loved her and who made her feel special.

For me, the highlight of the evening came after the meal had ended. Edna was tired and asked to lie down, but she wanted us to continue on with our fun. She would take her little rest on my couch, so she could listen to our conversation. It made me warm inside to know that Edna was comfortable enough around us to have her rest, and to just be herself in my house.

Comfort in Edna

My visits with Edna continued when she moved to Columbia Forest. I always rejoiced in the chance to be with her—to talk with her, laugh with her and benefit from her wisdom. She was the type of person that you could trust totally; a person you knew would never betray a confidence. The day I found out that I had cancer, I visited Edna and cried. She stroked my hair and comforted me, just as my own grandmother would have done in such a situation. She told me that I would get better. And so I did.

When Edna's health made a turn for the worse in early September, I wanted to be there for her, as she had been for me in my crisis. As usual, even when she was ill, Edna was upbeat, very lucid and rational. She said to me, "I told myself, 'Well Edna, you know it's going to end for you some day,' but, I didn't think it would end quite like this."

During that visit, Edna asked me to go over to her curio cabinet which stood in the corner of her room. It held many of the treasures that she had collected over the years. She asked me to pick out something that I liked—a keepsake that would help me remember our friendship. Edna never said things like this in a "poor me" tone of voice. She was matter-of-fact, and knew that for her, the end was near.

My choice was a small decorative milk jug that had been made by a Mennonite craftsman. Edna said that it had always been a favourite of hers. And now, I often look at that little milk jug and rejoice that I was able to know Edna as I did, in the last years of her life. Her friendship was a gift far more precious than she might have known.

Teresa Huegel
Waterloo
March 2007

Edna:
The Neighbour

We make our friends, we make our enemies;
but God makes our next door neighbour.

G.K Chesterton

Edna:
The Neighbour

Bonnie Koppelin and Marilyn McClement (nee Angst)
"Mrs. Staebler was one of those people that children just naturally gravitate to."

Jack and Mardi Kersell
"By the time Edna was in her 80's, her driveway was like a parking lot!"

Kevin Thomason
"If I heard and owl hooting or saw the large herd of wild turkeys...I couldn't wait to tell Edna about it....and she was the same."

Yvonne (Bonnie) Koppelin and Marilyn McClement

From 1941 to 1954 the Angst family lived at 45 Simeon Street, just two doors down from Edna and Keith Staebler. Like many in the neighbourhood "gang," sisters Yvonne (Bonnie) and Marilyn Angst could often be found, after school and on holidays, at 51 Simeon visiting the kindly Mrs. Staebler. As honeybees are to flowers, as kittens are to a warm lap, the youngsters of Simeon Street were drawn to the magnetic personality of Edna Staebler.

Even after they married and left home in the early 1950's, Bonnie and Marilyn followed the growing literary fame of their former friend and neighbour. For Bonnie, at least, her path would not cross Edna's for another 40 years.

Now in their 70's, Bonnie Koppelin of San Jacinto, California, and her sister Marilyn McClement of Scarborough recall memories of their childhood, and of a very special neighbour.

We all loved Mrs. Staebler—both boys and girls. She was one of those people children just naturally gravitate to. It was probably because she was so friendly and open. She'd take time to listen to us, no matter what silly things we had to say. It was always chatter, chatter, chatter between her and us kids. When I think back on our time in her company, the memories are always of great fun Mrs. Staebler just wasn't like other adults. She seemed to know how to get the best out of youngsters.

Birthdays were even better with Mrs. Staebler around. Thinking back on it now, she must have kept track of who had a birthday and when, because it seemed that she was always throwing parties for someone at her house. They'd be on a Saturday, at lunch time, and always involved the kind of food that little kids like.

I have one really special memory of her taking me on my birthday to the Doon School of Fine Arts. [1] It was my very first time in an art museum, and I think my lifelong interest in art probably got its start thanks to the wonderful Mrs. Staebler. We followed the trip to the gallery with a bit of shopping. Oh I felt so grown up! But the best part of the day was having Mrs. Staebler all to myself, instead of having to share her with the other kids. She was just so wonderful and fun.

Marilyn McClement
Scarborough, Ontario
January 2007

1. The Doon School of Fine Arts in the Doon area of Kitchener was renamed The Homer Watson House & Gallery.

Bonnie Koppelin's recollections of Edna Staebler call to mind a beloved cat and a grand piano.

Mrs. Staebler was a real cat lover, and she had this handsome cat. I don't recall his name. Now she absolutely doted on that cat, which had the shiniest coat I'd ever seen. But it wasn't until she hired me to baby sit him, while she went away to write one of her stories, that I realized how well-loved that cat really was.

Before Mrs. Staebler left, she showed me how to cook fresh liver, which she had bought at the butcher shop for her cat. It had to be cooked and cut "just so," and she made sure that I understood how to do it. No cat I ever heard of had fresh-cooked liver every day! I felt proud that I was the one she'd picked to take care for her cat. It made me feel very grown-up and responsible.

Mr. Staebler's Piano
The neighbourhood gang didn't get to know Mr. Staebler nearly as well as Mrs. Staebler. He worked during the day and didn't have the time to spend with a bunch of little kids. But we would

know when he was home from the sound of a piano coming out of their windows.

Now having a piano was no special thing, but Mr. Staebler's piano was. It was a beautiful Grand. We'd never seen one like this before! He played divinely, and especially in the summertime, when the windows were open, the sounds would drift throughout the neighbourhood. It was wonderful—like in a dream, and I'd often drift off to sleep listening to those sweet sounds. But this story gets even better!

When some of the great musicians came to Kitchener for concerts, they'd often make their way back to Mr. and Mrs. Staebler's house for informal "jam sessions." Now these were not just any musicians, but great names such as Duke Ellington and Louis Armstrong. Even though the music might go on into the wee hours of the morning, who would complain about having a free concert from the likes of these big stars!

Oh these are such pleasant memories from so, so long ago.

A Chance Meeting in the Country

Around 1991, my husband Wray and I were visiting Kitchener on a holiday. We'd made plans to eat at the Heidelberg Hotel, which was owned by one of Wray's relatives. During the meal, he came over to our table and mentioned that the famous writer Edna Staebler had just come in for lunch. It seems that his establishment was one of her favourite places for good, old-fashioned Waterloo County cooking.

I mentioned to him that Mrs. Staebler (I still thought of her that way!) had been a neighbour on Simeon Street. I guess he must have told her I was here. Imagine my surprise and delight when Edna came over to our table. She knew me right away, and asked about Marilyn, who had always been so special to her. We chatted for awhile, recalling old neighbours and old times.

I was struck by how little she had changed since I had last seen her 40 years ago. Still friendly, kind, and attentive, she made you feel that that you were special; that what you had to say was the most important thing going on in the world right now.

Several weeks after our return home to California, I went to the mail to find a package sent from Waterloo. Inside was a copy of Edna's best-selling cookbook, *Food That Really Schmecks*. I opened the book to find an inscription inside.

"To Bonnie, whom I knew when she was my neighbour, Yvonne. Edna Staebler."

I treasure it still. So lucky we were to have known Edna Staebler—a great writer; a better friend.

Bonnie Koppelin
San Jacinta, California
January 2007

Jack and Mardi Kersell

When, in 1964 Edna moved to the Sunfish Lake cottage that she and Keith had built some years before, she gained a new neighbour and reconnected with an old acquaintance. Mardi Robinson had first met Edna in 1951 through Keith Staebler. Mardi's (then) husband Wally was an alcoholic, and in desperation, she'd contacted Alcoholics Anonymous. The organization offered to connect one of their present members with Wally to offer support. That person was Keith Staebler.

Now, Kitchener-Waterloo was a small town in those days, and most people knew each other's business. Everyone knew that Keith Staebler had a drinking problem, and had joined AA himself. He'd volunteered to become a sponsor to new AA members. He'd come to our house to talk to Wally when things were going badly. Occasionally we'd go over to his and Edna's house on Simeon Street.

Keith was a terrific guy and had many, many friends around town. He was a gifted pianist and played at private and public functions. Everybody thought he should have become a professional. But like most of us, Keith had his bad points too. On top of the drinking, he was irascible, a womanizer and a *prima donna*. He craved the spotlight and when it wasn't on him, he was unhappy. People knew what a rough life Edna had. An incident that happened one time when we were visiting them showed just how rough it could be.

By this time, Edna had just started writing for *Maclean's Magazine* and was developing a career of her own. This just didn't sit well with Keith, although, to be sure, their marital problems had started long before Edna was a published writer. During the visit, the talk turned to Edna's writing and she happily welcomed the attention. Keith suddenly bolted up, went over the piano and started to play it so loud it drowned the conversation out. Talk of Edna's writing stopped then and there! It's funny, but despite this kind of stuff, Wally and I thought the world of him—a lot of people did.

Just Not "Well-Mated"

Edna and Keith just weren't mated. Most of their friends wondered why they had ever married. But they stayed together for years—probably because of their status in the community. Divorces were so rare in those days and in a small place like Kitchener-Waterloo, it was pretty-well unheard of.

So when it got out that Keith wanted a divorce from Edna, it caused quite the stir. Then when people found out that he wanted to marry Edna's best friend Helen Kergin[1]...; well, you can just imagine what *everybody* was talking about.

It was an ugly situation and Edna was devastated. Losing Keith was one thing; losing him to Helen, a person she had taken into her home was a humiliation. Edna felt betrayed, and well she should have. I had adored Keith but after this, I had trouble being civil to him. He had just treated Edna so badly.

I was happy for her when she sold the house. It had bad memories and she needed to get on with her life—far away from Keith and Helen.

Serene Sunfish

Edna and Keith had needed to "go in the back door" in order to build their Sunfish Lake cottage. In the 1950's, a man named Albert Wilson owned much of the land around the lake. He'd only sell lots to couples with children. Wilson felt very strongly that a lake was to be enjoyed by children, so if you didn't have a family, you didn't get to live at Sunfish.

Wally and I did, and we built ours in 1954.[2] Edna and Keith didn't have kids, but Edna's sister, Norma (Norm) and her husband Ralph Hodgson did. So I believe that the land was originally bought in Norm and Edna's names. I think that the Hodgsons intended, at one time, to build there themselves. When Keith and Edna built, the cottage remained in Edna's name.

Talking it Out

It took Edna some time to get straightened around after the divorce. Friends helped a lot during this time in her life. She gained a lot of strength too from a discussion group that we both belonged to at the time. Several of us met once a week to discuss ideas and philosophies. Edna didn't say much about the Keith-Helen situation, but she did talk a lot about the Cape Breton Island book that she'd been writing for years. It never seemed to get finished.

I can remember during one of these discussions, someone suggested that Edna either "get on the pot or get off," regarding the never-ending book. And you know, I think we inevitably helped her "get off the pot." Eventually, it did get finished.[3]

In the late 1960's, Mardi and Wally Robinson divorced. Mardi met her second husband, Jack Kersell, a Political Science professor at the University of Waterloo, in the mid-1970's. They married in 1981 and moved permanently to Sunfish Lake. No longer just weekend neighbours, the Kersells and Edna now saw each other more frequently. By this time, Edna was firmly in love with her lakeside home and entertaining guests regularly.

Many of Edna's visitors were writing friends from Toronto. These "big city" types enjoyed getting away from it all at a quiet, secluded lake. Pierre and Janet Berton and their whole brood of kids were there from time to time; and sometimes writer Scott Young and his family. Pierre was a big guy, both in terms of his size and personality. He'd walk over to visit with us from time to time, and we liked him a lot.

As Edna aged, she seemed to get more visitors. By the time she was in her 80's, her driveway was like a parking lot! I think she welcomed more visitors in a week than most of the rest of on the lake put all together! We joked to her that if she charged a parking fee, then she'd be able to retire early. Edna liked that.

But one day I was over talking to her and she complained that nobody had come to pay a call the previous weekend. You could tell that Edna didn't like this situation one bit. She was lost without people calling on her. I jokingly told her that if she had followed through on my suggestion about the parking fee, she could encourage her callers to show up on the weekends by offering free parking.

More Car Stories

It was probably a good thing that Edna stayed home as much as she did because she was a "terror" behind the wheel. She seemed only to know two speeds—fast and faster. You always knew when Edna was leaving, or returning home from the sound of the brakes of her car screeching, and gravel flying.

I'm not sure she ever used her rear view mirror either, because she'd pull right out in front of you. Nobody was safe when Edna was behind the wheel. I'm telling you more than one person was relieved when she gave up her car at age 97.

Loss of an Old Friend

We knew Edna for many, many years—good years and bad ones. We went through a lot together, but were never in each other's pockets. In fact, we really didn't see each other all that often. Still a year after her death, we miss her terribly. To us, she was never "Edna Staebler, celebrity" and we never put her on a pedestal. She was just Edna, our good friend and neighbour.

Jack and Mardi Kersell
Sunfish Lake
June 2007

---

1. Edna and Keith sheltered Edna's university friend, Helen (MacDonald) Kergin and her son after Helen's divorce in 1959. Details of this event may be read in Veronica Ross's *To Experience Wonder: Edna Staebler; A Life* (Toronto:

Dundurn Press, 2003).

2. Mardi and her husband Wally used the Sunfish Lake property only on weekends and vacations.

3. After working on the manuscript for over twenty-five years, Edna Staebler's *Cape Breton Harbour* was finally published in 1972.

Kevin Thomason

Kevin Thomason moved to Sunfish Lake in 1994, and in purchasing the former Playford house he became Edna Staebler's next door neighbour. Being single and in his 20's at the time, his interest in the small house caused a bit of a stir in the tight-knit, mature and privacy-seeking neighbours, including Edna. They worried that their idyllic Sunfish Lake might become "party central."

In an unusual process, his offer to buy the home was contingent on him being interviewed by his prospective neighbours, and winning their acceptance and approval. Step one was undergoing a "grilling" by the imposing Bill Henderson, the spokesperson for the other Sunfish Lake residents. The second step was attending a dinner meeting for a "look over" by the larger Sunfish Lake community. It was at this function, that he first met his prospective next-door neighbour, the legendary Edna Staebler. She was then 88 years old.

Finally judged by the group to be acceptable—having respect for the environment, agreeing to hold no loud parties or owning a noisy, powerful motor boat— Kevin was deemed an acceptable prospect for a neighbour, and the house deal closed.

Thus begun a close friendship between the Kevin and Edna, that only ended with Edna's death. Thirteen years after his move to Sunfish Lake, Kevin looks back on his days with Edna.

Edna and I got to know each other first through proximity. When you live out in the country and run out of milk or need a letter posted, you don't jump into a car and drive into town at the drop of a hat. So if I was going into town to do errands, I'd ask Edna if there was anything she needed. And she did the same. It was neighbourly to do things like this, and I guess you could say that Edna and I were very good neighbours.

Edna Behind the Wheel
I always knew when Edna was returning to Sunfish and coming down the laneway by the roar of the car and the cloud of dust

she kicked up. Age meant nothing to Edna. At 90, she had more energy than many people have at 50. And she drove like she did everything else—at top speed, raring to go.

Watching Edna zoom away made me think of stories that I had heard about Belle Playford, the original builder and owner of my house. She and Edna were great compatriots. Belle was a widow and, with Edna, was one of the Sunfish Lake pioneers in the 1960's. In the winter, the road into the lake wasn't always well cleared (sometimes not cleared at all). After returning home from work, Belle would park her car out on the Wilmot Line, strap on her snowshoes, pile her groceries on a toboggan and strike off over the hills to her house. The next morning, she'd do the same to get back out to her car.

Being a writer, Edna's schedule was less strict than Belle's, but winter was winter at Sunfish, especially in those early days. And so she needed to be self-sufficient to endure. Sometimes during spells of particularly nasty weather, Edna could go for days, maybe longer, seeing no one. Thank goodness for the telephone which would ring continuously with friends and fans checking in to see how she was faring.

A Common Love for Nature

Helping each other out with chores, errands, work around the house and meals was not the only bond that Edna and I shared. We both carried with us a deep love of nature and a respect for the environment. Edna and I would constantly marvel at the ever-changing waters of Sunfish Lake; the creatures which we'd see daily, and the woods that surrounded us.

We loved to share stories about the most recent sighting of a bird or animal. Sometimes it would be a quite common creature such as a rabbit or cardinal; other times, it would be to share news of more elusive animal, such as an otter, osprey, even a coyote or deer. If I heard an owl hooting, saw the large herd of wild turkeys, or ran across an unusual salamander or newt by the lake, I couldn't wait to tell Edna about it. And she was the same.

Edna loved nothing more than a refreshing lake swim on a warm summer morning. But of course, she never did things half way. Where most swimmers might have paddled out a few feet and back, Edna would swim right to the middle of the lake. And Sunfish Lake is deep—very deep. I was always a bit nervous for Edna and tried to convince her to swim around the edge of the lake, closer to residents' docks. Of course, I really never needed to worry. Edna knew her boundaries. She continued to swim right up to her final summers at Sunfish.

Making a Decision

By the summer of 2003, age was finally creeping up on Edna. She was 97 years old. Still, she accomplished things people decades younger would never consider. And many people couldn't keep up with her—Edna of the "always walk quickly" style of movement.

Only in her mid-90's did she give up her car. Her license was still valid and her driving record clean. She'd tell visitors: "I only put 40 miles on the car last year, and this seems like a pretty expensive 40 miles, given the cost of gas, maintenance and insurance." And so the car had to go. Where many would have feared isolation in relinquishing this link to the outside world, Edna had few concerns. From my home next door, I gave witness to how little this decision affected her.

So now the world came to Edna. Not that they hadn't before, to some extent. Sunfish had always been a favourite spot for so many of Edna's friends and fans. But now, the steady stream of visitors grew. There were few days that at least one car didn't pull up to her driveway. And between folks dropping by, the many phone calls and the large amount of mail that came to her mailbox every day, Edna was never lonely.

After all visitors were gone, I'd often drop over for a few minutes, just to make sure she was fine, and to ask if she needed anything from town the next day. It's just what neighbours do in the country; neighbours look out for, and help one another.

The World Comes…and Comes Again

I've often thought about why so many people came to visit Edna. It certainly wasn't obligation or a sense of duty. Edna had visitors because people wanted to be there. But why? I think it was because she was so interesting, so compelling. Edna always had so much more to offer a conversation than talk of her health. She was different than most elderly people in this way.

You could also learn so much from her; she was wise and had experienced life. Edna had traveled widely, met and become friends with interesting people, and had done fascinating things herself. She'd also experienced challenges and pain in her lifetime. Edna was so very "real." You never left her without learning something new, or carrying a "nugget" of wisdom with you. No, conversation with Edna Staebler was never dull.

Still, Edna was no showoff. Nor did she demand that the conversation be "all about me." Quite on the contrary, Edna was beloved because she was so engaging. She loved people and was genuinely interested in what *you* were doing in *your* life. If you had pets, Edna wanted to know about the pets; if you were back from a trip, Edna was "all ears" to hear about this. You'd just finished a good book? Edna wanted your opinion on it. And it wasn't superficial. Edna really wanted to know.

So Grateful

And finally, there was gratitude. Edna was always so grateful for her visitors. She would tell each and every person who came to call how glad she was that they had dropped by. She was thankful for things that people did for her. Even when she wasn't feeling well herself, with a toothache that would have sent most people to their beds, Edna still showed her delight in welcoming people to her home.

No person was ever turned away from Edna's door. Nor did anyone ever see her angry, or complaining, or even "down in the dumps." She'd often wonder aloud what good things were going to happen in her life that day. And before the day was done, she'd tell you what those good things had been.

Stories to Share, Lesson to Learn

Edna knew that she wouldn't live forever. But before that finality, she had many lessons that she wished to impart. And I had so many things I wanted to learn from her. So our days passed in this way. On her part, Edna would share memories of experiences, people and history. She'd tell stories of the invention of electricity, telephones and the first automobiles. All had been in their infancy in the early years of this century, when Edna was born. I had my tales too of the latest technology— of Blackberries and Palm Pilots and other wizardry. And so, we learned from each other.

I've always felt fortunate that I knew Edna as I did—as her next-door neighbour, and later her friend. I'm lucky, as well, to have had the opportunity to spend the time with her that I did. With 64 years between us in age, we were so different in many ways. Still, we brought unique experiences and perspectives to our friendship.

An Easy Choice to Make

Occasionally, as is the case with most of us, there would be times that I needed to choose between two events going on at the same time. Maybe it was going out to a party, a movie or a social event with some of my same-age friends. Or, I could be escorting Edna to a play, a dinner or a reception. For me, it was always an easy choice. I could go out with my friends another time. I might not have the opportunity to be with Edna again.

Even now, it's difficult for me to grow accustomed to the empty cottage beside mine. One day last summer, I went outside to find a huge snapping turtle sitting on my back step. My initial thought was: "I've got to tell Edna about this." And then I'd remember— "Edna's not there." Just the other day I got in my car and as I turned the bend in the road, a herd of deer crossed. I counted 22 of them. "I've got to tell Edna"…and then I remembered.

Yes, I miss Edna. We all do.

Kevin Thomason
Sunfish Lake
March 2007

Edna:
The Philanthropist

*We ourselves feel that what we are
doing is just a drop in the ocean. But if that
drop was not in the ocean, I think the ocean
would be less because of that missing drop.*

Mother Teresa

Edna: the Philanthropist

Dr. Robert Rosehart
"I had also learned that the sweet elderly lady in the red sweatshirt was a shrewd bargainer. Edna Staebler was a tough as nails about money."

Scott Hayter
"It was great publicity for the university, a fitting tribute to Edna. And we plan to continue to be noisy about it every step of the way."

Joe Mancini
"I'm sure I was tongue-tied and incoherent, but I must have asked if I could know the identity of the donor. The man told me it was Edna Staebler."

Kim Jernigan
"We were astounded. It was a significant amount of money for a little magazine like ours."

Judith Miller
"She appreciated books on the Second World War, marijuana, birds railway travel, canoeing…"

George Blackburn
"Edna inspired him and he felt very comfortable sharing thoughts and opinions with her that he might otherwise have more closely safeguarded."

Tom Allen

"A warmth, an energy seemed to radiate from her, and passed to me. I felt it in my chest, in my heart and lungs, and I immediately felt a connection to her."

Linda Johns

"I can't see any bunny without recalling our Edna-Rabbit, queen of the studio. Do you remember the 'card' that she sent you?"

Dr. Robert Rosehart

One of the early missions that Dr. Robert Rosehart took on in 1997, when he succeeded Dr. John Weir as President of Wilfrid Laurier University, was to visit Edna Staebler. It seemed that certain issues had arisen regarding the Edna Staebler Award for Creative Nonfiction which the university administered. A visit to Sunfish Lake was advised as soon as the new President had gotten himself settled.

Ten years later, and now retired from the Presidency of WLU, "Dr. Bob" recollects the memorable day when he and his administrative assistant Beth Harrison first traveled to Sunfish Lake. It would be a journey they would make many times over the next 8 years.

Soon after I took up my post as President, I was told about Edna Staebler. Edna was what I'd call a "curiosity person" at WLU. She was also an important donor and it was necessary to keep her happy. When I arrived on the scene, it appeared that she wasn't.

There were two issues at hand. One was financial. It appeared that the Staebler Award was short of money. Either the amount given each year would need to be reduced, or Edna would have to put more money into the fund. That seemed pretty straightforward, to me, at least.

The other situation was somewhat more complex. It surfaced that the dealings between Edna and the previous administration had been way too formal for Edna's liking. I'd been advised to pay a *social* call on her early, to smooth the waters. I hoped I could combine the two visits in one.

I immediately liked Edna and conversation between us was easy. My mother was around the same age as Edna at that time—91—so I could relate well to her. We talked about other topics that interested both of us, before I brought up the money issue. That conversation went well and I left feeling that much had been accomplished.

It wasn't until I was driving home that it struck me what really happened over the course of our conversation. I had come out to get more money from Edna for the Award; I had left a couple of hours later promising to cover the shortfall *myself*! From the President's budget! And 10 years later, the President's Office still tops up the Award—every year. I fixed that problem alright!

In the course of the afternoon, I had also learned that the sweet, elderly lady in the red sweatshirt was a shrewd bargainer. Edna Staebler was as "tough as nails" about money. I learned too that when she had made her mind up about something—especially when it involved money—nothing was going to budge her. You did it Edna's way or no way, and that toughness was carried through to the last days of her life.

Thinking Young

As I got to know Edna better, I concluded that she didn't really act her age, if there is such a thing. She didn't "think old" or "act old," so people didn't see her as old. She drew much of her energy from the youthful and vibrant people who surrounded her. I might even say Edna was "turned on by youth."

And yes, Edna could be flirtatious. There was always a definite twinkle in her eye when a man was around. "He keeps coming to see me," she'd say of her male visitors. Nor was she shy about talking about her past loves—her trips to Paris and other European cities. It was clear that she had enjoyed men in her youth. And she remained a vibrant woman well into her 90's.

President's Choice

Trips to Sunfish, whether on business or pleasure, or a mixture of both, always came with some refreshments—served by the hostess. In the early days, Edna usually served us scones and tea. Then one day, our conversation turned to blueberries. I told her that I loved blueberries; that I had indulged in my passion for them at Lakehead University[1] where blueberry pickings were common "rites of summer."

So the next time we went to visit Edna, she served us blueberry muffins. And oh! were they tasty! I joked to her that these really should be called "President's Choice" muffins, after the popular Loblaw's brand. This really caught her fancy, and from that time on, a visit to Sunfish was never complete without the "President's Choice Blueberry Muffins."

I'm aware that some people think that I laid waste to Edna's plate of muffins on more than one occasion. I've heard the numbers up to 12 in one sitting! That's an exaggeration, but I do admit to enjoying 8 or 10 of them, at least once. Apparently Edna and Beth would calculate the relative deliciousness of the muffins on any given visit by how many were left on the platter after I left. Whatever the number, I wish to say, in my own defense, that Edna's muffins were *small*.

At Edna's memorial, which was held at WLU after her death, blueberry muffins were included in the refreshments served to mourners. Apparently, the staff at the university commissary had somehow secured Edna's recipe. It was a personal reminder for me of the unique bond between a very special individual and this university.

And no; I don't remember how many I ate on that day.

Robert Rosehart
Waterloo
January 2007

---

1. Dr. Robert Rosehart was President of Lakehead University before he assumed the same role at WLU in 1997. He retired in August 2007.

Scott Hayter

In early May of 2007, several days after the announcement by the Waterloo Region District School Board that a new school would be named in honour of Edna Staebler, another large piece of "Edna-news" was made public. Edna had made a $1 million bequest to Wilfrid Laurier University. The significant donation would be directed towards developing young writers at the university as well as increasing the support Edna already gave to established Canadian writers.

Scott Hayter, WLU's Assistant Vice-President, University Development, had worked with Edna's advisors in the winter of 2006 on the conditions of the bequest. He speculates how Edna's generosity will benefit writers for years to come—both within the university community and for writers across Canada.

I first met Edna at her 100th birthday celebration, in January 2006, which was held here at WLU. As newcomer to the community, I hadn't had the privilege of knowing her previous to this. But, of course, even before I took up my position I was well aware of who she was, and of her generosity to Laurier.[1]

Meeting her at this occasion was telling. Not only did I get a sense of her own generosity of spirit and personal warmth, but I was able to see first-hand what the community thought of her. It was clear that people loved Edna.

Some time after the birthday party, I received a call from her lawyer. It was the type of message that all people who work in positions like mine like to receive. Edna had made a bequest to the university of $1 million. Her representative invited me to meet to discuss the details. It was an extraordinary piece of news, but it would need to remain very quiet for the time being until all the "i's" were dotted, and all the t's were crossed."

Over the next few weeks the specifics of the bequest were worked out, although most of the details had already been addressed long before I received the call. Edna's friend, Kathryn Wardropper had worked hand in hand with her to develop a well thought-out, and meticulously detailed bequest. I was extremely impressed with its clarity and thoroughness.

Part One of Edna's Bequest

There were two parts of the endowment: one was directed at the university itself; the other was in regards to the Edna Staebler Award for Creative Nonfiction.[2] This latter award was a national writing award, but had been administered by WLU since its inception in 1991. Edna now directed $250,000 of the total bequest in this direction. Her wishes were that this amount would be used to increase the award's dollar value from $3000 to $10,000 annually, commencing with the 2008 winner.

When I learned this detail, I called to mind part of the conversation that Edna and I had had at her birthday celebration. She had spoken to me then of the impact that winning the Canadian Women's Press Club Award had had on her own writing career back in 1950.[3] "It gave me the confidence to continue on with my writing," she told me, and added that when she set up her own award in 1991, it was done in the same spirit.

Edna knew how much the Staebler Award had meant to the writers who had won it, because she had met and talked to each of them. She had heard their heart-felt thanks from their own mouths. It was so obvious to me then, from the sparkle in her eyes, how much Edna loved being the vehicle to help, in this way.

And now she could help even more. Edna felt that by increasing the dollar value of the Staebler Award, she could create a more prestigious recognition. And this might encourage more young writers to take up the craft.

And then....Part Two

The remainder of the monies—some $750,000, would be used to establish the Edna Staebler Writer-in-Residence Program. Her wishes were as clear for this arm of the bequest as they had been for the other.

Where the Edna Staebler Creative Nonfiction Award was directed at already-established Canadian writers, the Writer-in-Residence program would target student writers. It would bring noteworthy Canadian authors to the university in an effort to develop and encourage creative writing on campus. At the same time, the position would afford the writer-in-residence the opportunity to pursue his or her own writing projects.

This seems, at first glance, like a very broad objective, but Edna's wishes were very specific on a number of points. She had clearly thought out how the writer-in-residence incumbent would be selected, and for what duration. She had given thought to what projects he or she would take on, and even what faculties throughout the university would be involved. While we are not entirely sure of Edna's rationale in this area, her wishes were that it would be interdisciplinary, excepting the School of Business and Economics.

High Praise for Clarity

Having worked with other benefactors at other universities, I could not have had higher praise than I did for Edna Staebler and those who advised her in making this bequest.

In situations where an individual bequeaths a large sum of money, clarity is always appreciated, and Edna's bequest was certainly clear. And for each specific term mentioned in the bequest, WLU was able to respond positively.

We had sat on our "big news" for almost a year, until all the details had been finalized. Then finally, in early May, 2007, we could make some noise about it. And we did! Our announcement made the front page in The *Record*. It was great publicity for the university, a fitting tribute to Edna. And we plan to continue to be as noisy as we can about it every step of the way!

Personally, I have only one regret with regards to Edna Staebler. I dearly wish that I had seized the opportunity to get to know her better, even so late in her life.

Scott Hayter
Waterloo
May 2007

---

1. Earlier, Edna had endowed the Gerry Noonan Memorial Scholarship to a deserving student studying English Literature or Film Studies at WLU, and the George Blackburn Memorial Scholarship for a worthy History student.

2. The Edna Staebler Creative Nonfiction Award is given annually to a Canadian author, writing in the Creative Nonfiction genre, (the literary genre Edna favoured in her own writing) for a first or second book.

3. Edna had won the Canadian Press Women's Award in 1950 for her *Maclean's*-published story, "How to Live Without Wars and Wedding Rings."

Joe Mancini

Joe and Stephanie Mancini founded the non-profit Working Center in 1984 as a resource center for Kitchener's homeless and working poor. By 2007, it has grown to 3 properties on Queen Street in Kitchener's downtown core, as well as St John's Kitchen, located on Victoria Street.

Both centers rely on government grants and community funding vehicles, as well as donations from charity events and individuals. Since 1987, its most high-profile fundraising initiative has been the popular Mayors' Dinner. This celebration honours individuals for their commitment to improving the lives of those less fortunate in their community.

The 2003 Mayors' Dinner held at Bingeman's Ballroom honoured Edna Staebler. This event provided the impetus for Edna's donation 3 years later of $25,000 to them. Founder Joe Mancini talks of meeting Edna for the first time in the fall of 2002 and later, of the dinner itself.

Each year, a committee meets to discuss who will be recognized at the Mayors' Dinner for the upcoming year. Past recipients have included some pretty high-profile names, including builder Peter Hallman, House of Friendship's Anna Kajalis, and former Kitchener Mayor Dom Cardillo. When someone suggested Edna's name, the committee unanimously agreed she would be a fitting recipient.

Neither Stephanie nor I had met Edna before the dinner, but, of course we had heard of her. We knew that there was a "mystique" around her and Sunfish Lake; we'd heard about the cookbooks, but unfortunately, we were aware of little more. But that would soon change!

After the committee had set their sights on Edna, Stephanie and I along with Board member Harry Froklage, who was a longtime Edna-friend, made our initial trip to Sunfish. The purpose was to sound her out about the proposed dinner.

Harry had told us on the way that Edna liked to be "engaged" in activities in which she took part. That meant she'd want to get to know us—what The Working Center and St. John's Kitchen stood for, and who *we*, Stephanie and I were.

Getting to Know You

Edna was delighted with the idea, and gladly agreed to being the Mayors' Dinner recipient. But once that formality was over, the conversation turned to other things, such as stories about Cape Breton; Edna's Mennonite friends; her trips for *Maclean's Magazine* and some of her friends, such as Pierre Berton and W.O. Mitchell. It was a magical afternoon for both of us. We were honoured to hear what we did that day.

I became fully entranced by Edna—this very old, rather frail lady, humble, yet confident, and vital, living alone in a modest cottage filled with books, on the shores of a little lake in the woods. I began to understand why so many people visited her and regretted that I hadn't known her long before.

But the talk that day was not all Edna-centered. We told her what she wanted to know about us and what we stood for and believed in. All this, and tea and cookies too!

We went home, knowing that we had met a very special person. We hoped we'd have the opportunity to visit with her again. I left anxious to read her books and stories and I looked them up. I was especially drawn to the articles she'd written about living with the Mennonites and also with the Italian community in Toronto.[1] With a last name of Mancini, it's probably easy to know why I was drawn to this one!

Several more trips were made to Edna's to plan the dinner's details. Harry was right. Edna did like to be "engaged," and she took full part in the talks. Her ideas were always good and sound. I was, as before, amazed and astonished by her.

As the day of the dinner drew closer, and more and more tickets were sold, we all knew it would be a full house—over

700 people. We were now learning how the community felt about Edna Staebler.

A Magical Evening, but...

It was a magical evening, despite some fairly serious glitches. The vegetables? Not cooked enough; some diners might have even said "raw." Emcee Michael Higgins, of St. Jerome's College quipped that he "almost cut (St. Jerome's President) Doug Letson's leg off with the chain saw they were using to cut up the potatoes!" The crowd roared.

And the microphone? Not working! Higgins to the rescue again, when he suggested that: "the only thing older in the room than Edna Staebler was Bingemans' sound system." The crowd, including the guest of honour, erupted again.

I don't think many in the audience took exception with these faults. When all was said and done, the Mayors' Dinner, 2003 version, was considered a great success. It had raised some much-needed money for us, and had honoured a very deserving recipient.

An Unexpected, and Much-Needed Gift

The year 2006 was shaping up to be a real time of growth for the Working Center. A third property on Queen Street had just been purchased, and we were undertaking big renovations for the St. John's Kitchen property. Coolers and stoves were needed before we could open. Money was so tight that we worried that we might not be able to make that first mortgage payment. Then a phone call came — a call that I won't soon forget.

The caller, a Kitchener lawyer, informed me that he was representing a donor who wished to make a "substantial donation" to the Working Center and St. John's Kitchen. He then asked me to give him the details of how a transaction of $25,000 could be passed from his client to us. I can't remember exactly what I said when I heard this; I'm sure I was tongue-tied and incoherent, but I must have asked if I could know the identity of the donor. The man told me that the benefactor was Edna Staebler.

To say we were overwhelmed is an understatement. To say we were grateful is not nearly enough. The timing of this gift couldn't have come at a more crucial moment. Divine intervention? I can't prove this, but to us, it was a prayer being answered.

In the days following the bequest, I gave more thought to Edna's gift. Not everyone sees the worth of what we do at the Working Center and at St. John's Kitchen. Call it "cultural snobbery." The idea of a "Soup Kitchen" brings up negative images for some people. But Edna had recognized our worth; she'd accepted that what we contribute to society is worthy, and then she'd contributed to it herself.

And we're not talking about a woman who was fabulously wealthy. Edna had lived simply and conserved her resources— much like the Mennonites whom she admired. The money which she gave away had been earned from her own pen; from her own skill as a writer. And when she had enough to support her needs until she passed on, then she gave it away to others who needed it. Was this not the purest form of philanthropy?

I gave thought, as well, to the timing of her bequest and congratulated her on the wisdom of giving when she was still living. How rewarding that must have been for her. Was Edna's giving not giving in the best possible way?

Joe Mancini
Kitchener
April, 2007

---

1. The article written by Edna Staebler, "Italian Canadians" was published in *Chatelaine Magazine*, March 1965.

Kim Jernigan

In 1980, Edna's friend Harold Horwood, who held the position of writer-in-residence at the University of Waterloo, spoke to Edna about his desire to see a literary magazine published in the Kitchener-Waterloo area. The two friends chipped in $1000 of their own money; writer Farley Mowat was convinced to add $1000 of his own. And so, The New Quarterly Magazine *was born.*

Through lean (and leaner) times, The New Quarterly *has featured fiction, poetry and essays, written by up-and-coming writers. Acclaimed Canadian authors, such as Jane Urquhart, Alison Pick and Andrew Pyper have also published in* TNQ. *Over the years, the magazine relied solely on a variety of private and public funds to put out its quarterly issue.*

A volunteer with TNQ *since its inception, Kim Jernigan took over from Harold Horwood as Editor in 1985. She has continued on in this position since that time. Working with her are a number of volunteers and a small staff, including Managing Editor Rosalynn Tyo. The magazine works out of a small office in St. Jerome's University, on the larger University of Waterloo grounds,*

Unexpectedly, in the fall of 2006, The New Quarterly's *ship came in.   Editor Jernigan recalls the circumstances:*

Edna had continued to have contact with the magazine after she, Horwood and Mowat got it off the ground, 25 years ago. She'd occasionally call the office or send a note if there was something she liked in a particular issue. Edna also tried to promote it when she could, and would pass the magazine on to other writers. She also allowed her name to be used in connection with a variety of fund-raising ventures which we headed up, including the "Edna Staebler Golf Tournament."[1]

We wanted to do a feature on Edna, and pegged it in for the Winter 2005 issue. By this time, she had moved to the Beechwood Manor Retirement Home. The plan was to include a recent interview that (writer and Edna's friend) Harry

Froklage had conducted with her, as well as parts of the 6-year long correspondence between Edna and her mentor Dr. John Robbins.

Edna had met Robbins in 1945 when he came to Kitchener to address the Canadian Club. He was a distinguished literary scholar and Professor of English Literature at the University of Toronto. Robbins had also recently won the Governor-General's Award for Literature, for his work, *The Incomplete Anglers.*

Between 1945 and 1952, when Robbins passed away, he and Edna became devoted "pen friends."

Edna's Wish is Granted

Edna had always felt strongly that the letters between her and Robbins should have been published. It was one of her great disappointments that no publisher had shown interest in it. I felt too that they were relevant. They showed a novice writer (Edna), experiencing remarkable growth over their 5-year correspondence. Beginning with uncertainty and self-doubt in 1945, she matured into a confident and respected journalist a few short years later. In the early letters, Edna is clearly in awe of Robbins. By the end, she's emerged as his literary equal. I believe that it's a fascinating example of Canadian literary history.

Our interest in the letters pleased Edna and she was eager to talk to us about our plans. We arrived at Beechwood Manor — my daughter Amanda, who is a contributing editor for *TNQ,* and her friend John Haney, a photographer. John's job was to photograph Edna for the cover of the magazine. Initially "ho-hum" about yet another picture taken of her, Edna's interest perked up once we moved outdoors to the garden.

The camera John was using was one of the old-fashioned "cloth over the head" ones. He loves the sharpness of the images it captures, plus he's always delighted by the crowd it draws when he sets it up. Edna was curious about it, and chatted to

John throughout the shoot. She even made a joke, guessing that: "the camera is probably even older than me!"

When the Edna Staebler issue—Number 93 Winter 2005 came out, it was warmly received by readers. Edna loved it too.

TNQ's "Ship" Comes In

Some months after the interview, I took a mysterious phone call. The caller said that he was representing a person who wished to make a significant contribution to *The New Quarterly*. He was telephoning to inquire what the procedure would be to do this. The man gave me no other information, so I had no idea who the donor was, or how much the amount was. Needless to say it was a very exciting time at the office!

Several days later, we received a letter that cleared up the mystery. The donor was none other than Edna Staebler; the amount of her gift was $25,000. We were astounded. It was such a significant amount of money for a little magazine like ours. Over the years, we'd never know if we'd have enough money to survive from one year to the next. So Edna's donation gave us some stability. It meant that we could do some things that we would never have been able to do otherwise.

We took time to decide how the gift would be used, but after considerable discussion among the staff and volunteers, we came to a meeting of the minds. Our first initiative will be an annual award of $1000 for the best non-fiction piece which has been published in the magazine for the previous year. We hope to have the winner selected by a celebrity judge. The genre of the piece of writing will be Creative Nonfiction. That of course was the style Edna wrote in herself. So it seemed a natural fit.

Secondly, we now can increase the stipend that we give to writers whose work is accepted by us. Regrettably what we or any similar magazine have been able to pay our writers in the past is a pittance when set against the writer's time and imaginative energy. Now, we can do better.

I'm sure Edna would have been pleased with these decisions, and we are so very indebted to her. She was so far-thinking in using her philanthropy while she was still living. Edna must have gained great happiness and satisfaction knowing how much she'd been able to help a cause that meant something to her. And what a wonderful legacy she's left.

Kim Jernigan
Waterloo
April 2007

---

1. The 2006 Edna Staebler Golf Tournament, played just after Edna's death, raised over $8,000.

Judith Miller

Dr. Judith Miller, Professor of English Literature at Renison College, University of Waterloo, poet and literary reviewer became a member of the Edna Staebler Award for Creative Nonfiction selection committee in 1993. She joined 6 others, including Edna herself, and the administrator of the award, Kathryn Wardropper.

Each year approximately 50 books, judged to have been written in the Creative Nonfiction genre are submitted by publishers to the committee. Over the coming winter and spring, each member of the group will read the books in preparation for discussion and eventual selection of the award winner.

The group traditionally met over 3 occasions in the summer at Sunfish Lake. Judith recalls the meetings as "lively, full of passionate discussion about books and writing, and the nature of Creative Nonfiction."

It is fun to imagine Edna's reaction to being described as a "critic." Certainly, she thought of herself as a writer and not a critic, and yet it is true that she was an insightful reader and an astute critic.

It was always a special pleasure to gather at Sunfish Lake with Edna and the boxes of books submitted each year to the Award. Edna, of course, was a wonderful hostess, and the tantalizing smell of freshly baked muffins met us at the door. There was tea or cold sweet cider to go with them, but we didn't get to eat until we had made a decision. It never occurred to me then that there was a strategy in that timing. We were always a very focused jury.

As we delved into the pile, which we had all read through, Edna commented enthusiastically on the books. She remembered small details from each one, where a character was especially vivid, or a situation was memorable. She had strong views about what constituted creative nonfiction. Edna believed that nonfiction became creative when it drew on the techniques of fiction, making characters alive, settings dramatic and language engaging. In addition, such a book needed a forward momentum that was not based on plot, but that drew the reader in to a series of events, ideas or characters that unfolded. A good book, in her opinion, captivated a reader. "I just had to keep reading this one..."

Edna's taste was eclectic. She appreciated books on the Second World War, marijuana, birds, railway travel, canoeing... "Oh, did you read this one?" she would ask, her face glowing. "I know it's not a winner, it's not really creative nonfiction, but the description of the lakeside was just perfect. It made me feel as if I were right there."

Accomplished writing delighted Edna, but she had no patience with the pretentious, the bombastic or the simply dull. She always preferred to dwell on the strengths of whatever she was reading, but she was firm about books that did not qualify for the prize—and her assessment was based not on subject matter but on weak structure or impenetrable writing. She thought that even the most complex ideas should be made accessible.

While Edna worked hard to match a book to the prize, she always listened carefully to discussions among the jury. "I learn so much from what you all say," she insisted. "I never would have noticed the science in this book, but Rick showed me how to appreciate it." As one among several of us on a jury of wide-ranging expertise, Edna offered her critiques. We tussled, until the group as a whole came to agreement about a prize-winner.

During the last meeting when Edna was with us, she was uncharacteristically quiet, saying little. When we had reached a conclusion, she confided privately, "I'm glad to know that I can still recognize good writing when I see it." Our choice was also her selection, it seems, as had often happened. It's hard to think about what it will be like to meet as a jury without Edna's lively presence and sound critical judgment.

Judith Miller
Waterloo
April 2007

Andrea Thompson and Kim Galway for George Blackburn

First as a Canadian soldier in wartime Europe, later as a composer, journalist, playwright, and radio producer, George Blackburn was a true "Renaissance Man." Yet he gained his celebrity late in life. The last of his three-part war trilogy, Where the Hell are the Guns? *was published in 1997, the year he turned 80.*

This book, as well as the previous two of the series, The Guns of Normandy: A Soldier's View *and* The Guns of Victory *became Canadian best-sellers.* The Guns of Normandy, *published in 1995 had brought him to the attention of Edna Staebler and the Edna Staebler Creative Nonfiction Award committee. He was named the winner of the 1996 Staebler Award for this book and earned the respect, admiration and friendship of its namesake.*

In November 2006, in Ottawa, George Blackburn passed away, a mere two months after Edna's passing. He was 89 years of age.

George's daughter, Andrea Thompson and his grand-daughter Kim Galway of Toronto offer their thoughts on the close friendship between the two.

There were several very important people in my grandfather's life. My grandmother, Grace was pre-eminent in his affections, but his dear friend Edna Staebler was also very special to him. Despite their physical distance from each other—he in Ottawa, Edna in Waterloo—they remained in touch by letter, phone call and at various functions they both attended. He and Grace would also make sure to drop in to visit Edna at Sunfish Lake, if business or pleasure brought them to the Waterloo area.

Perhaps it was because they were both literary late bloomers; perhaps it was their shared passion for their craft; in any case, my grandfather George and Edna were fast friends. They shared, too, late recognition by their country for their talents and achievements. Both were invested into the Order of Canada. Edna's honour came in 1996; George's in 2001. In 2004, France honoured him with the esteemed Legion of Honour.

So proud of George's achievements was Edna that in 2000 she endowed the George G. Blackburn Memorial Award for Canadian History at Wilfrid Laurier University. She felt that it was a fitting tribute to a man who had contributed so much to Canadian letters, most prominently in history.

Grace's death in April 2002 shattered my grandfather. Edna's ability to philosophize and speak in deeply intellectual and creative dimensions really helped him find solace following her passing. Edna inspired him, and he felt very comfortable sharing thoughts and opinions with her that he might, otherwise, have more closely safeguarded.

Edna's creation of the George Blackburn Award for History at Wilfrid Laurier University touched him very deeply. I recall him sharing the news of this honour with pride and a profound sense of honour.

My grandfather was one of the most stoic people I ever knew, yet as his health deteriorated near the end of his life, much of his suffering was done so silently that others weren't even aware of it. Traveling away from Ottawa was something he rarely did. But when the invitation came for Edna's 100th birthday celebration in Waterloo, nothing could have prevented him from attending.

He promptly booked his train from Ottawa to Kitchener for what I know must have been an exhausting journey. He felt compelled and was most delighted to attend such a monumental benchmark for his precious friend.

Kim Galway
Toronto,
August 2007

I remember both Dad and Mother enjoying Edna's tremendous artistry at letter-writing. I recall too their delight in receiving a print of the painting of her that had been created.[1] They displayed it proudly on their living room wall, already overcrowded with sentimental artworks from dear friends. Edna's image took a place of honour above Mother's chair.

They took tremendous happiness in, and felt quite honoured when Edna included them in her "inner circle" of special friends. Her invitations to her beautiful lake home resulted in them returning home full of stories of astonishment at her sense of humour and her vast range of interests. They admired too Edna's sharp intellect and her ability to think creatively. So too did they appreciate the ease by which Edna could philosophize, injecting love and enthusiasm into all her doings—despite her advanced age.

A trip to visit with Edna resulted in my parents returning home with newly-injected momentum to live life to its fullest and to the very end.

My father's determination to attend Edna's 100th birthday in Waterloo came despite the physical disabilities with which he now struggled, as a result of a recent stroke. He now had difficulty speaking clearly. Yet, he maneuvered through the complexities of communication which such a journey would involve.

And when he got there, his piano playing (which miraculously had been left untouched by the stroke) thrilled Edna and her friends before he left to come home.

Andrea Thompson
Toronto
August 2007

---

1. The painting that Andrea refers to is the one created by Peter Etril Snyder.

Tom Allen

Tom Allen of Toronto won the Edna Staebler Award for Creative Nonfiction in 2002. His book Rolling Home: A Cross-Canada Railroad Memoir[1] *presented the stories of train passengers, railway workers and Tom's own adventures on the train, intertwining them with snippets of Canadian rail history. He is also the author of* Toe Rubber Blues: Midlife Thoughts on the Prospect of Aging. *Tom Allen's latest book is* Gift of the Game: A Father, A Son and the Wisdom of Hockey. *Also an accomplished musician, Tom has hosted CBC Radio 2's "Music & Company" since 1998.*

Winning the Edna Staebler Award came for Tom at a time of personal transition. He looks back on it, and his subsequent meeting of Edna Staebler as "pivotal and hugely meaningful" in his life.

Whenever I think back to the day that I found out that I had won Edna's award, I remember how close I had come to losing my life! I was out in my driveway trying to put up a basketball hoop. My cell phone rang and I stopped what I was doing to answer it, right there in the driveway. My back was facing the hoop which was attached to a heavy board.

No sooner had I said hello than the hoop came crashing down right beside me. If I'd been a meter further left it would have struck my head, probably killing me. I think that I was in a state of shock when the caller told me I'd won the Edna Staebler Award for Creative Nonfiction. I sure don't remember much about that conversation.

But everything that came after that was good—especially the opportunity I had at the award banquet in Waterloo to talk to Edna. Now, I must confess, that I knew very little about her or her accomplishments before we met. I knew that she wrote cookbooks, and was quite old. Period. But I did my homework before we met, and found that I had sorely sold her short on her accomplishments.

Expecting to find a doddering old lady—I don't think I had ever met a person that old before—I met instead this warm, vibrant and caring person, still very much in charge of her faculties.

How can I explain the way Edna Staebler affected me at that first meeting? It was a feeling quite unlike anything I had had before—or have felt since. A warmth, an energy seemed to radiate from her, and passed to me. I felt it in my chest, in my heart and lungs and I immediately felt a connection to her.

During our chat that evening, she spoke of her own early days writing and the disappointment she had felt at her family's disinterest in her accomplishments. I saw her willingness to open her heart and soul to me as a precious vulnerability. Edna had made a conscious decision to trust me, and I felt honoured. I left that evening hoping that I'd be able to hold that trust.

Just Like I Imagined
My next meeting with Edna was at Sunfish Lake the next spring. And, as I knew it would be, her cottage and where it stood were just like Edna herself—warm, kind, and cozy. It was an almost magical place with the tall pine trees, the clean, clear lake, the squirrels and birds and other wild creatures. And indoors, a cozy cottage, full of books, paintings, photographs and treasures. Some were very old and all were a precious part of Edna's own memories.

I remember that what affected me most that day was seeing the painting by Linda Johns on Edna's living room wall. Linda had won the Edna Staebler Award for her book *Sharing a Robin's Life*[2] several years before me. As I looked at her art, I felt such a connection—her to me, me to her, both of us to Edna. It was a magical moment. I didn't want to leave that day because then the spell would be broken.

Bringing Family
I didn't see Edna again until 2005, after she had moved to Beechwood Manor Retirement Home. This time I brought with me my two young daughters. I very much wanted them to meet her. We had made plans to pick Edna up in Waterloo and take

her out to Sunfish for a visit. It was a beautiful day and we were all looking forward to it.

The girls were so excited when we arrived at "the woods." While Edna had some quiet time inside with her books and her cat, Mally, the kids and I enjoyed the beautiful out-of-doors. We swam in the lake, played Frisbee, watched the birds and the chipmunks and just soaked in the peace of nature.

After awhile, we joined Edna in the house. Again, like I had felt before, there was a deep connection to her as I entered into her world. We hadn't been inside long when someone else came to pay a call. I recall a feeling, almost of jealousy, that came over me as Edna turned her attention to the caller. "These precious moments belong to me, not you," I said to myself, hoping the interloper might take his early leave.

We left for home that day relaxed and re-energized. I hoped that it would not be the last time I would see Edna. But it was.

Edna's death affected me as a great, personal loss. I felt I had always known her, when in fact it had been only a short 4 years. And when I look back on the marvelous human being who was Edna Staebler, one word comes to mind. That is "magnetism." While others blessed with the same trait might use such power for selfish ends or to seek riches or control, Edna's magnetism was all good, pure and kind. Hers was a life that sought its meaning in relationships. I was so lucky to have been able to return the same, in kind.

Tom Allen
Toronto
December 2006

---

1. Tom Allen, *Rolling Home: A Cross-Canada Railroad Memoir* (Toronto: Viking Canada, 2001).

2. Linda Johns, *Sharing a Robin's Life* (Halifax: Nimbus Publishing, 1993).

Linda Johns

Linda Johns of James River, Antigonish County, Nova Scotia won the 1994 Edna Staebler Award for Creative Nonfiction for her book, Sharing a Robin's Life. *Known in her region of the province as "the Bird Lady," Linda is a practicing sculptor, painter and illustrator, as well as the author of 11 other books. Most of these chronicle her adventures with the many woodland creatures that share her home, studio and heart. One, a rabbit named Edna, with a predilection for chewing on the spines of books was a particular favourite of both Linda and the rabbit's namesake, Edna Staebler.*

Over the years, following Linda's selection as Staebler Award winner, and up to Edna's death in 2006, she and Edna carried on a regular correspondence. Often Linda's letters would entertain Edna with anecdotes and the continuing adventures of the "rascally rabbit."

In paying tribute to Edna, Linda has chosen a letter to offer her reminiscence of her friend.

Dear Edna:

I've been asked to write about our years of correspondence and friendship, a seemingly straight-forward request that left me staring out my desk window day after day. I watched birds and squirrels busily hulling seeds, late sunlight gilding leaves, a spider weaving a web — intimate sights that we both savoured daily and shared in our letters. Yet writing about writing each other remained, in the end, un-writeable. So I decided instead to write a last letter to you, Edna.

I know you'll be glad that the baby pigeon battered by the crow is making a strong recovery. At this moment, he's sleeping contentedly in my lap, his once bare and bloodied back fully feathered, wings and tail lengthening each day. His confidence has really grown, yet whenever he hears a crow cawing nearby, both eyes become round with fear and he tries to hide in the bookcase. Some wounds never heal. I wish crows preferred tofu. It sure "Schmecks" for us!

Your stories about the squirrels you see from your window are always delightful. Baby squirrels are out on their own here, too. We see them not only in the seed boxes but climbing up bushes to eat honeysuckle and wild elder blooms. They've already eaten enough apple blossoms to lower our expectations of apples in the fall, but who can blame them? Something that smells that good has to taste even better.

There's one youngster that worries us for although his head, legs and tail are furred, his tiny squirrel body remains bare. Maybe you could take a moment from knitting mice to make him a sweater!

Yes, Mack's garden is doing very well. You recall the 4 groundhogs that feasted in it last year? They won't succeed this year. Mack has constructed a running maze of fenced plots guaranteed not only to protect the veggies but to defeat any groundhog that isn't also a structural engineer. It almost defeated me as I tried to make my way to the rhubarb patch in hopes of having a hot pudding for dessert tonight.

I watched a couple of bunnies, round eyes and tall ears rising above the jack-in-the-pulpits. One of them, I suspect, snipped off my nodding trilliums. Is your bunny still coming to the back door in the evenings?

I can't see any bunny without recalling our Edna Rabbit, queen of the studio. Do you remember the card she 'sent' you? And the photo of you in your red jacket, but with long black ears, like our Edna's? It seems only yesterday that she was a frightened baby rabbit that we were teaching to use a litter box. I'll never forget the look on Jeff's face when I galloped into Lyghtesome Gallery and blurted out, "Guess what, Jeff! Edna isn't peeing on the floor anymore!" Of course he thought I was referring to you and positively howled when he realized

I meant the rabbit. You—to your credit!—howled even louder when I told you that story on the telephone. Confusion is bound to arise when a rabbit is named after an acclaimed friend.

Mack's raccoons camp on the doorstep every night—15 lactating mothers! Big Momma this year has only two. As you know, she and her last litter of 4 were featured on the Solstice card we mailed you. Despite her bad experience last summer, Chunk had babies again, though we don't know how many yet. Moonface, however, vanished last fall. In 2 or 3 weeks all 15 will be bringing their families and Mack will be out on the doorstep distributing cookies to a new generation.

Most of our porcupines are still coming nightly to the kitchen window feeder for their cracked corn. Last evening Mack lifted the sash and Oreo pushed his head right inside, let Mack rub him on the nose, then gently accepted an apple. But he dropped the apple in favour of corn when Mack poured out a full scoop. "Porkies" are such lovely animals and their fur up close is wonderfully rich.

Glad to hear that lots of books are arriving for your award in the fall, and that there's such variety in the topics. Your summer reading will be well taken care of, as usual. I've been re-reading Jane Austen and Virginia Woolf—old favourites that just keep getting better. I also dipped into the Owl Pen books again and I know how much you like them too. The Owl Pen honey pot is on my desk as I write—another reminder of your generosity. And your handwoven wool poncho covers the bed, glowing with colours.

I must close, Edna. A big whalebone carving needs to be sanded before the show, and afterwards I'll take photos of all the new carvings for you. I'm glad you liked this past winter's paintings. I felt they broke through to a new threshold, which is always encouraging. As for the rejected manuscript, you've heartened me. I'm going to send it to another publisher.

I'm enclosing a gorgeous blue jay feather that I picked up, and a sand dollar from the beach for you to invest! Glad you enjoyed the Newfoundland postcards. Isn't the landscape there awe-inspiring?

All best wishes from us both, Edna, and know that we think of you each day.

Linda, Mack, and the creatures

Linda Johns
James River, Nova Scotia
June 2007

Edna:
The Latter Years

*To keep the heart unwrinkled, to be
hopeful, kindly, cheerful, reverent
—that is to triumph over old age*

Thomas Bailey Adrich

Edna: the Latter Years

Ruth Deyarmond
"… it soon appeared that Edna was different, at least in one way, from most residents."

Bob and Sheila Chaffecombe
"But was Edna ever mad at me when I told her who I'd turned away! But she got over it and we remained friends."

Cathy Greico, Shalagh Cassidy and Michaele Hajkova
"After the (birthday) party, she seemed so very, very weary…"

Ruth Deyarmond

After a stroke suffered at home in May 2003, Edna moved to Beechwood Manor Retirement Home on Erb Street in Waterloo. Both Edna and those closest to her hoped that the relocation would be a temporary one. Edna made the best of the situation. She eased into life at the pleasant Beechwood Manor, making friends and participating in social events planned for residents. But the hi-light of each day for Edna was greeting the steady stream of visitors who arrived at her door.

Administrator of Beechwood Manor, Ruth Deyarmond, recalls her staff's reaction after news of Edna's arrival was made known.

Of course, as a staff we were honoured when we heard that Edna would be coming to Beechwood Manor. It was exciting to know we would have a celebrity here. But at the same time, it was important that Edna not be treated any differently than any other resident—that there not be any favoritism shown. We worked hard to make Edna feel one of our community.

However, it soon became apparent that Edna was different, at least in one way, from most residents. She usually had more visitors in one day than some residents might have in a week— or even month. Most of her guests came singly; others arrived in groups. Regularly, a group of her Old Order Mennonite friends came to call, usually bringing lunch or supper. They made it clear that this was no reflection on our food. Their gesture was just a measure of caring for Edna. We never thought ill of this; in fact we thought it a charming custom.

Edna never discouraged the steady stream of visitors, even though they clearly tired her out. This soon became a concern to us. Staff were protective of her, and we took the responsibility of caring for her seriously, as we do everyone who lives here. We felt that it was in Edna's best interests to discourage callers from arriving after lunch, and put up a sign on her door asking them to respect her need for a nap between 1pm and 3pm. And most visitors abided by it; the few who didn't, we suggested strongly that they come back another time.

At first Edna was quite resistant to the idea, but in time she learned that she did pay the price for too much socializing. She began to learn her limits. Where before she could "go go go," now she realized that she just didn't have the stamina. A very busy or eventful day would be followed the next by exhaustion. Still, if it had been left to her, Edna wouldn't have traded every last one of her visitors for anything. This is what kept her going.

No Airs; No Fancy Clothes

Never did we get the "I'm a celebrity" attitude from Edna. She treated everyone the same. Nor did she monopolize conversations, with other residents or with staff with too much talk about herself. I began to notice that Edna often opened most conversations by saying: "tell me about you; tell me about what is going on in your life." She knew that everyone had a need to tell their own stories, and she enjoyed hearing them. As I came to know her better, I understood that, in part, this selflessness was why so many people wanted to visit her, why so many people cared.

Neither did Edna put on airs, materialistically, although I know she had the financial means to. Like most elderly people, comfort in clothes was more important than style, and Edna wore track suits most of the time. Her favourite was a red one—well-worn, having seen better days. When Christmas approached, some of her visitors asked us if there was anything we knew that Edna needed. We suggested that a new track suit or two might be welcome.

Come Christmas, that's what Edna got—several of them. And they went right into her closet and stayed there. Edna preferred the old red one!

A Stubborn Reluctance

Edna was very capable when she moved to our facility, and she needed little assistance to move around. But then her legs began to fail her and she resisted using a walker or wheelchair. In fact, I'll say that she was pretty stubborn about acknowledging her diminished physical capacity. When we found her on the floor after a fall, it shocked her. She realized, for the first time, that she needed more help.

So, Edna's friends and family began looking for a facility that would meet her needs more fully. In February 2005, she left Beechwood Manor. We all missed her, and some staff were quite heart-broken about losing her. For myself, I felt very fortunate to have known Edna Staebler, even for a brief time.

In looking back on her time with us, I'm reminded of a quotation by humanist Albert Schweitzer. He said: "We all live spiritually by what others have given us in the significant hours of our life." I think that Edna gave so much, to so many people, in what *they* will remember as the significant hours of their own lives.

Ruth Deyarmond
Waterloo
April, 2007

Bob and Sheila Chaffecombe

Bob and Sheila Chaffecombe's introduction to Edna came at Joseph Schneider Haus. Sheila was working as a teacher-interpreter at the popular Kitchener museum and Edna, then 85, had been invited to speak to an audience there about her famous Schmecks *cookbooks.*

The Chaffecombes, big Edna fans, were front row centre. Bob, who had just celebrated his 40th birthday, had with him several copies of the Schmecks *series. He hoped to have them autographed by the author.*

Still exuding the charisma, good humour and sharp wit that had endeared her to audiences for decades, Edna was in fine form for the appreciative crowd. An impromptu comment to Sheila about an article of clothing that she was wearing was the unlikely jump-off point for a connection that would span two eras of Edna's life.

I was wearing a sweatshirt that read: "Owner of the World's Cutest Cat." As soon as Edna noticed it, she corrected me by saying: "No you're not; I'm the owner of the world's cutest cat!" It gave us all a laugh—the first of many we'd have that night. I guess, it also established a bond between the 3 of us. We were all crazy about cats!

After the talk was over, we took Bob's cookbooks for autographing. He was "on the moon" about meeting her, and she couldn't have been more approachable when we went up to her. Here was a celebrity who acted just like ordinary folks. It was impossible not to adore Edna, right off the bat.

Bob's Salmon

Our next contact with Edna came a few years later. I had found a recipe for baked salmon in one of her books and wanted to try it. Only the instructions didn't include how long to cook it. I was doing it for a special occasion, so didn't want to ruin it. I guess it was remembering how friendly she'd been at Schneider Haus, but I decided to try to contact her to ask for her cooking advice.

How to do this was another matter. We didn't think such a famous person would have her phone number in the book. But there she was. Edna Staebler, R.R. #3, Waterloo! So I called, introduced myself and asked my question.

Edna must have had a few people visiting, at the time, because she hollored back into the room: "Anybody know how long to cook that salmon?" I heard some voices in the background offering an opinion and she reported back. I realized then how naïve my question to her had been. This was someone who knew hundreds and hundreds of recipes. And I expected her to know the answer to my question right off the bat? I was a bit embarrassed and apologized.

No matter how silly I felt, Edna didn't think so. She told me how grateful she was that I'd called and said that she liked knowing that people were trying her recipes. I'd had a high opinion of her before. Now it was even higher.

Doing Some "Crowd Control"
Sheila's path crossed with Edna Staebler's again in 2003. She was now working as Care Attendant at Beechwood Manor Retirement Home, and the buzz around the building was that Edna Staebler was coming there to live.

The staff at Beechwood were excited that Edna was going to become a resident. Some had met her informally like me, but most would be meeting Edna for the first time. We'd heard what a popular person she was, and how many visitors she'd entertained at Sunfish Lake. It wasn't too long before we found out how popular she *really* was.

From the very first day, Edna had large numbers of visitors—many, many more than other residents. At first, we thought it would drop off after she'd been here a few weeks, but no. Never a day would go by without several people—some singly; some in groups arriving.

She thrived on this company; that was obvious by her smiles and laughter. But it didn't take us long to realize that the constant entertaining was tiring her out too. We knew that she would never suggest to anyone that she needed some quiet time during the day. So for Edna's sake, *we'd* have to do some crowd control.

We instituted a rule that Edna would have her rest time right after noon meal. Her door would be closed to visitors between 1:00 and 3:00 pm, and we put a sign up on her door saying that.

Most people obeyed the rule, but occasionally a person who perhaps didn't know about it would show up. That happened one early afternoon with the President of Wilfrid Laurier University, no less—Dr. Robert Rosehart. I saw him come in and head towards Edna's room. I stopped him and politely asked if he might be able to return another time. Edna was having her rest. I wondered if he'd be angry, but not at all. He'd come back later in the day.

But was Edna ever mad at me when I told her who I'd turned away! But she got over it, and we remained good friends.

A Cape Breton Connection

Some of our family lived in Cape Breton Island and we had begun to think about moving there. I shared this with Edna and she was thrilled for us. Cape Breton was one of her very favourite places on earth. From then on, each day when I came in to see her she'd tell me bits and pieces about her Cape Breton adventures.

When Christmas came around I arranged to be Edna's "Secret Santa." I had a special Cape Breton gift that I wanted to give her. I'd bought a dark green sweatshirt for her—Edna loved sweatshirts—and had sewed a heart with the Cape Breton tartan on the front. Edna loved it, and it didn't go into the closet with most of the other clothes people brought her![1]

The Cat Connection

Our first contact with Edna 12 years before had come about because of cats. So it was no surprise that Edna and I would often share cat stories. Our cats are a bit unusual—Sphinxes, the hairless variety. Every once in awhile I'd bring one of them, Rana, into work to visit with the residents. She was friendly and loved to sit on laps, including Edna's.

Talk of cats would sometimes make Edna sad. She had left her own cat, Mally, behind at Sunfish and she missed Mally terribly. One day, I arrived at work and learned that Mally had died. I immediately went to talk to Edna and it was the only time I ever saw her cry. I held her hand, and we talked about her loss.

But by the next morning, she had processed Mally's death and was her usual self. Never selfish; never thinking of her own loss; but grateful for her years with Mally. Edna was at peace, too, that her cat had been able to die in the only home she had known.

Sheila Corrects an Oversight

After our move to Cape Breton, we continued to keep in touch with Edna who was now at Columbia Forest Long Term Care. After her passing, a very small article about her connection to the island, specifically to Neil's Harbour, had appeared in one of Cape Breton's two newspapers. I thought that it was poorly done—small and stuck in the middle of the paper somewhere.

Considering what Edna had done for Neil's Harbour and its schools, and feeling protective of Edna, I thought it needed to be better. So I contacted the newspaper and complained about the oversight. They followed up by doing a phone interview with me, and then wrote another article which paid due respect to her.[2]

I think back on our friendship with Edna and see it as one of the very good things in our lives. To have met, shared stories with, and near the end, assisted Edna Staebler was a privilege. We were blessed to have known her.

Bob and Sheila Chaffecombe
Sydney Mines
Cape Breton Island
April, 2007

1. Beechwood Manor Administrator, Ruth Deyarmond tells an anecdote about what usually happened to Edna's gifts of clothing elsewhere in this book.

2. The improved obituary is included in the picture section at the back of the book.

Cathy Greico, Shalagh Cassidy and Michaela Hajkova

Edna moved to Columbia Forest Long Term Care in Waterloo in April 2005. Her failing health had necessitated more care than had been available at Beechwood Manor. Columbia Forest proved be an ideal location for her; it was close to Sunfish Lake, and it boasted two resident cats. Both would ease Edna into her new address.

The staff at Columbia Forest adjusted themselves also to having a celebrity in their midst. And while Edna neither expected, nor demanded different treatment than any other resident, her popularity presented some challenges, as it had at Beechwood Manor.

Several staff played an integral part in making Edna's time there as happy and fulfilling as it could be. Cathy Greico, a Registered Practical Nurse supervised Edna's medical requirements and her medication; Shalagh Cassidy, Columbia Forest's Program Manager invited Edna to participate in recreational programs; and Michaela Hajkova, a Personal Support Worker attended to Edna's physical needs, such as bathing and hair care. They recall their time with Edna fondly and feel privileged to have been able to assist her in the final months of her life.

But, Edna's connection to Columbia Forest would not be complete without the story of the last feline love of her life—Oliver.

Cathy Greico, R.P.N.

When I look back on my time with Edna, it's not her curiosity, or her wonderful personality or her kindness that I remember most. It's her great romanticism that stands out above all.

Now that might surprise some people, given that her own married life was not a happy one. But Edna did have love in her life. She talked to me about the Swiss man that she loved, and told me about the beautiful picnic that they had one day with the Alps in the background. I thought how much in love she must have been, because her eyes sparkled when she told the story.

But it wasn't just love in her own life that made Edna a romantic. It was love in other people's lives that delighted her too. Especially when she had had something to do with it! Edna wasn't a gossip, but one day she was bursting to tell me how, through visiting her, two singles had met and found love. This just made Edna burst!

Shalagh Cassidy, Program Manager

I was constantly amazed at the agility of Edna's mind. It showed itself in so many ways—not the least would be her interest in flowers. People were always sending her or bringing her bouquets of flowers. Everyone knew how much Edna loved them, and she'd always direct anyone's attention to the latest delivery when they came into her room.

But where many people might have smelled their fragrance and noted what was in the bouquets, Edna paid real attention to the flowers—the variety, the colours and the size. And if there was a type of flower that she wasn't familiar with, she'd want to find out. Often she'd ask me because I was interested too.

On these occasions I'd talk to my mom who was an avid gardener, and report my findings back to Edna. So I became the "flower expert" in the same way that Michaela was "the poet." I soon found out that for Edna, learning never stopped. There was always new information to take in, even if it was a little thing like the variety of a flower.

I think that's one of the reasons why people loved to visit her. She had so much to talk about and was interested in so many things. For me, I couldn't wait till I had the opportunity each day to drop in to say hello.

Edna still kept her sense of humour too and could be quite funny. On the days leading up to her 100th birthday she received hundreds of cards, letters and almost as many bouquets of flowers. I was in her room when she received a spectacular bouquet from her M.P.P. She opened up the card and commented: "Well she's a lovely woman, and has nice taste in flowers, but I could never vote for her—the party's wrong!" I guess Edna was a Liberal!

Michaela Hajkova, Personal Support Worker

When you work in a job that has you assisting people in their most personal needs, you often develop a strong bond with them. So it was with Edna and me. We soon realized that we had a very special bond; this was a love of literature. I write poetry, and from time to time I'd bring some of my poems in for Edna to read. She always encouraged me to continue writing; she told me that what I was writing was good. This meant so much to hear these words coming from a person like Edna. Soon, I came to think of her as my muse. In turn, she allowed me to read some of the entries in her diary. I was honoured by her trust in me.

Edna was different after she had her 100th birthday party. It seemed that she had been holding on, being strong for that, because she knew how much it meant to so many *other* people. And after the party was over she seemed so very weary. She just "let go." We all thought that she had made her peace with life and was now ready to die. But there was one thing she had to finish first: *The Da Vinci Code.*

She had been reading it for awhile and told me that although she was intrigued by the story and the ideas in the book, she thought that it was written poorly. Each day we talked about it, as I had read it too. I think both of us looked forward to our daily discussion of Dan Brown's best seller.

In the last days before her death, it became too great an effort for her to hold the book up and read the words on the page. But she was determined to finish it, so each time I came into her room, I read some to her. With only 11 pages of the book left to read, Edna suffered another stroke and passed into a coma.

I wondered what to do. We had started a journey together and I knew she would have wanted us to finish. So I sat by her and read aloud the last few pages. I have no doubt in my mind that Edna heard every word I read before she passed away. It was such an emotional time for me and I will always feel very grateful that I was able to do this for Edna at the end of her life.

Oliver the Cat

When Edna moved to Beechwood Manor in the spring of 2003, she left her cat, Mally behind. The cat would be cared for by Edna's neighbours, and the tenant who was living in her cottage. Still she looked forward to periodic trips back to Sunfish for visits with her beloved pet.[1]

When it became evident that Edna needed to move to a facility that offered more care than Beechwood, her family and friends searched out alternatives. Not only did Columbia Forest in northwest Waterloo fit the bill for proximity to Sunfish Lake, but it also offered a bonus. Two housecats named Hooper and Oliver lived there.

Columbia Forest staff talk about the strong bond that grew up between Edna Staebler and the handsome Oliver.

Oliver had always been fairly distant with most residents. He might drop in to see someone and stay for a day or so, but he usually hung out under the Nurses' Station desk. This changed when Edna arrived.

Whether it was because he liked the catnip mice that she knit, or whether it was something about Edna's voice or personality, but within days of Edna arriving, Oliver had become a one-woman cat.

From then on, Oliver's territory was Edna's room. She kept cat treats and toys for him there and always welcomed him to sit on her lap—all 17 pounds of him—when she was watching television. When Edna had her afternoon nap, Oliver slept on her bed.

A Traitor in the Midst

Then one morning when Edna woke up, Oliver was nowhere to be found. Around lunch time, he strolled into her room, got a liver treat, then left. Edna was concerned. Then we found out the reason for his disappearing act.

Apparently, a new resident, also a big cat lover had been "bribing" Oliver with better treats than Edna had been giving him. So he'd decided to stay—at least for awhile. When news of this reached Edna, she was not amused. Someone reported that they'd heard her say: "Well, something's going to be done about *that*." We never knew what Edna did to get Oliver back, but within a day or so he'd returned "home."

When Edna fell into a coma, Oliver remained on her bed. He lay beside her when she passed away. For days after this, he lay in the doorway of Edna's former room. It was so clear that he was waiting for her to return. When a new resident moved in, Oliver left.

He remained in mourning for weeks. Now, he only wanted to be in his basket under the Nursing Station where he'd stayed before Edna came. Nothing tempted him. He refused treats and ate only a bit of food. Even stroking him didn't seem to make him happy.

In time, Oliver became more like his old self, but still a year after Edna's death he hadn't found someone to take her place. Edna was an impossible act to follow.

Cathy Greico
Shalagh Cassidy
Michaela Hajkova

Waterloo
October 2006

---

1. Mally died while Edna was at Beechwood Manor.

Photographs

Edna's graduaton photo from the University of Toronto, 1929.

Edna 1956, age 50.

Livvy Kraemer's "little black recipe book."

Livvy Kraemer and Edna c. 1970.

Edna and friend Barbara Naylor
in front of Edna's cottage.

Sunfish Lake, October 2003

Painting which Edna kept in her bedroom
to warn against "fear".

*Edna's transportation to the Castle Kilbride Party
- a 1938 Rolls Royce Wraith.*

Old friends, Pierre Berton and Edna.

Dr. Gerry Noonan.

"Cookie War" lawyer
Michael Manson.

Chauffeur
Minas Vassiliadis.

Edna wearing her
Order of Canada.

Edna and Livvy Kraemer in their mid-90s.

Peter Etril Snyder's portrait of Edna
(hangs in Kitchener Public Library).

Janet Berton, Edna and George Blackburn.

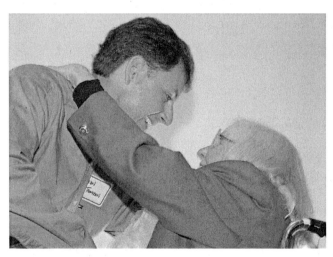

Edna and Kevin Thomason.

BRETON

FRIDAY, SEPTEMBER 15, 2006

CAPE BRETON POST

Late author loved Cape Breton

SYDNEY MINES – Edna Staebler had a deep affection for Cape Breton that lasted long after she published a book about the Neil's Harbour area in the 1970s, a former caregiver of the author says.

Staebler, regarded as the author who brought Mennonite cuisine into homes across Canada with the cookbook she wrote, died this week at the Ontario nursing home where she spent the last three years of her life.

Sheila Chaffecombe worked at Beechwood Manor Retirement Lodge in Waterloo while Staebler resided there. But she had come into contact with Staebler even earlier, as the author would give lectures at a Kitchener museum where Chaffecombe once worked.

"I was one of the fortunate ones to look after her, we had an amazing rapport," Chaffecombe said. "What a wonderful lady."

Now when she thinks about Staebler, Chaffecombe recalls her warm smile and cleverness, how good a good friend she was to people and her love of cats.

When Chaffecombe and her husband subsequently moved to Cape Breton to be closer to their grandchildren in Sydney Mines, Staebler told her she was living her dream.

"She was always in love with Cape Breton," Chaffecombe said. "I believe she travelled in the '40s to Cape Breton, wrote her book in the early '70s. Every time you talked to her about Cape Breton, she came to life even more."

Aside from cookbooks, Staebler wrote historical non-fiction, including Cape Breton Harbour, published in 1972, about life in the Neil's Harbour area.

Prior to her foray into books, she was a journalist who wrote for Maclean's and Saturday Night magazines and a number of newspapers in the 1940s and '50s.

Staebler was awarded the Order of Canada in 1996.

Notice of Edna's passing from the Cape Breton Post.

Edna at Columbia Forest with Oliver.

Selected Bibliography

Books by Edna Staebler:

Cape Breton Harbour. Toronto: McClelland and Stewart, 1972; reprinted by McGraw-Hill Ryerson, 1990.

Food that Really Schmecks: Mennonite Country Cooking as Prepared by My Mennonite Friend, Bevvy Martin, My Mother, and Other Fine Cooks. Toronto: McGraw-Hill Ryerson, 1968.

Haven't Any News: Ruby's Letters from the '50's. Ruby Cress; edited by Edna Staebler. Waterloo: Wilfrid Laurier Press, 1995.

More Food that Really Schmecks. Toronto: McClelland and Stewart, 1979.

Sauerkraut and Enterprise. University Women's Club of Kitchener-Waterloo, 1967; Toronto: McClelland and Stewart, 1969.

Schmecks Appeal. More Mennonite Cooking. Toronto: McClelland and Stewart, 1987.

The Schmecks Appeal Cookbook Series (series of 12 cookbooks). Toronto: McClelland and Stewart, 1990.

Whatever Happened to Maggie and Other People I've Known. Toronto: McClelland and Stewart, 1983; reprinted as *Places I've Been and People I've Known: Stories from Across Canada*. McGraw-Hill Ryerson,1990.

Periodical Articles by Edna Staebler:

"Duelists of the Deep." *Maclean's Magazine*, July 15, 1948.

"How to Live Without Wars and Wedding Rings." *Maclean's Magazine*, April 1, 1950.

Between 1948 and 1993, Edna Staebler wrote fifteen feature-length articles for *Maclean's Magazine*. She also wrote six feature length articles for *Chatelaine* and *Saturday Night Magazines*; the *Toronto Star Weekly* and *The Old Farmer's Almanac Canadian Edition*.

Others:

Berton, Pierre and Berton, Janet. *Pierre and Janet Berton's Canadian Food Guide*. Toronto: McClelland and Stewart, 1974. The Bertons' book was originally published as The Centennial Food Guide in 1966.

Ford, Anne Rochon. *A Path Not Strewn with Roses; One Hundred Years of Women at the University of Toronto, 1884-1984*. Toronto: University of Toronto Press, 1985.

Ross, Veronica. *To Experience Wonder: Edna Staebler: A Life*. Toronto: Dundurn Press, 2003.

Silcox, Nancy. *Roads of the Heart. Fifty People Who Followed Their Passion*. New Hamburg: Once Upon Your Memory Publishing, 2002.

Verduyn, Christl. *Must Write: Edna Staebler's Diaries*. Waterloo: Wilfrid Laurier Press, 2005.